Wings of My Father

By
Andrew Angelo

PAGE PUBLISHING, INC.
New York, NY

First originally published by Page Publishing, Inc. 2017

ISBN 978-1-64082-645-8 (Paperback)
ISBN 978-1-64082-646-5 (Digital)

Printed in the United States of America

A tale of a documented real emergency flight of November 15, 1971, flown by the author as a young corporate chief pilot. The emergency flight of 1971 is told to a flight crew by the author during an actual flight while he is acting as a captain of United Airlines flying from Boston to London.

The actual flight flown by the author in 1971 in the twin Aztec as a young corporate chief pilot is based on his vivid recollection of that flight while being supported by the telling of the rescue efforts by actual FAA transcript written that day.

The names of the occupants of the Aztec, Captain Angelo and Charles Califf, are of course actual as are the author's family members. The other names are a composite of individuals that the author has had the privilege of knowing and working with during his extensive aviation career and are not the actual names of the individuals depicted in the story.

All efforts employed during the air rescue attempt are based on actual actions taken by the rescue team with the obvious unknown actual conversations that took place being based on the author's interpretation of their actions during the flight.

Any names or characters mentioned, other than those listed as actual in this book, are coincidental and are not based on a specific individuals known by the author.

CHAPTER 1

THE ORIGIN

Summer 1947

I was a four-year-old boy walking with my father along the boardwalk at Revere Beach, just outside the greater Boston, Massachusetts, area. It was a warm summer day, and we slowly strolled hand and hand with no intentions, but the pleasure of being together to enjoy the sounds, sights, and smells of the ocean front along with the exciting atmosphere of the beach's activities.

"Look..." My father pointed to a distant object slowly descending from the sky. "That's a DC3 landing at Boston's airport." I was awed by the distant craft in the sky and wondered how it stayed in the sky.

"Daddy, how does that stay in the air?" My four-year-old mind could not conceive of the concept of flight, but my father explained to me the mechanics of flight. My father had just a basic understanding of flight, and he did his best to reason with a four-year-old on the theory of flight.

"That's an aeroplane. The wings and propellers make it fly like a bird."

I smiled up at Daddy and received a huge warm smile. He quickly picked me up and twirled me around by my arms while making the sounds of an aircraft engine.

I was flying through the air on the wings of my father's powerful arms, feeling the movement of the wind in my face. I was in absolute joy and contentment in this simulation of flight made possible by my father. He quickly threw me overhead into the air, releasing my hands. I flew…I flew!

He snatched me out of the air and laughed as he hugged me. "Little man, you flew like a bird!"

CHAPTER 2

SHUTTLE FLIGHT BOSTON TO NEW YORK

Spring 2000

"Captain…" A gentle touch on my shoulder brought me out of my dream world. "We're landing in a few minutes. We need to put on your seat belt."

I was on the air shuttle from Boston's Logan Airport to New York City's La Guardia airport.

"Sorry, I was sleeping and didn't hear the announcement."

The pretty young flight attendant smiled at me. "Have a fun night last night?"

"No, getting a little old for being a bad boy."

She was being kind when she remarked, "You're not so old, Captain. Where you headed tonight?"

"Jolly Old London Town…1900 out of JFK."

She bantered back, "Whew, must be nice to be a United International captain. I know our shuttle pilots are envious of the pilots at United."

I nodded and shrugged to end the conversation and the FA walked away smiling at me. The dream had not left me completely, and I still sensed my father's presence in my mind and soul. I had started to dream more of Pop, his later years' name and attributed it to getting older. Christ, I'm fifty-seven years old, almost twenty years older than my father in my dream. I missed him and couldn't believe he had died twenty-two years earlier from the ravages of Parkinson's disease. A solid man of almost two hundred pounds of muscle with iron hands reduced to a shell long before his time should have ended. He was captain of his high school football team, an all-around athlete proud of his strength and physique. He was a rugged construction worker who came home from the dirt of cement and work with clean clothes and body.

The Parkinson started very early in his life at forty-five years of age and slowly destroyed his body until he died at the age of seventy.

I often dream of him where I am a boy, and he is young in his years before the Parkinson's had started to show on his body and its movements.

I like to attribute my love of aviation to the joy of that day so long ago and my pop throwing me around as if I were flying. I can still feel the rush of wind and the thrill of spinning in the air on the wings of my father.

We were in the approach phase of the flight into New York La Guardia when the thought of having to hustle over to JFK via a taxicab ride during rush hour commuting gave me pause for not commuting to New York the previous night. I was mad at myself for not following the routine of disengaging all nonaviation activities at least twenty-four hours before report time at United in order to clear my mind and physically get ready for the flight.

I liked the routine of spending the night on the island in solitude and getting in a run and work out at the local fitness center prior to the two-hour report before flight departure time at JFK; family affairs demanded a same-day commute and report for flight.

The shuttle flight landed with a thud, and I mockingly remarked to myself, "Nice landing."

I found a cab in record time, and we set off for JFK. I was extremely happy that the driver knew the location of the United's operation's building off the main entrance road to the terminals. It took about thirty minutes and a quick exchange of money and receipt had me walking into the front door of OPS.

CHAPTER 3

FLIGHT 996

The main floor was packed with flight crews arriving and departing for flights. There was a loud buzz of conversation throughout the room as I made my way to my inbox to check for company notices and aircraft or navigation manual revisions. A rapid successions of "how's it going" to fellow pilots led me to the "flight dispatch desk."

I was greeted by, "Evening, Captain, what flight number?"

I replied, "Flight 996 to London," while I read through the laid-out dispatch papers.

I heard a familiar voice shout out to me, "Hey, Captain Angelo, you flying with me?" I turn to see First Officer Joe Messina and shouted back, "No, you're flying with me!"

The flight dispatcher gave me a quizzical look. I quickly quipped, "Have to set the FO straight before they get too familiar." First Officer Messina walked over with his hand extended and a grin ear to ear on his face. We exchanged handshakes and said, "Glad I'm flying with you tonight," before proceeding to go over the flight papers. Dispatch release, flight plan, weather reports, weather forecasts, fuel sheets, maintenance release, aircraft equipment status, and a myriad of required signatures before we could set off to the terminal to board our Boeing 767-300.

I really like Joe, a redheaded Italian American with roots in New England. I was glad to have him working the fight with me this evening. He was an above average pilot and first officer with plenty of flight time and experience under his belt with a good sense of humor. I had been flying out of NY for about ten years, and I liked the flight personnel based here due to our similar backgrounds. We met our relief pilot required for flights over eight hours, Frank Bell. We exchanged greetings, and he quickly left us to go to the departure gate at the terminal. Neither Joe nor I knew him, but that was not unusual as at that time UAL had over ten thousand pilots and New York was a fairly large B767 base. While we walked to the gate from our crew bus, I told Joe I wanted to do the preflight walk around of the aircraft and for him to set up the cockpit for departure. This was a reversal of roles for the first phase of preparing for departure.

Joe gave me a look. "Okay, you're the boss."

I grabbed him. "Yeah…don't forget it!"

It was a warm late April evening, and it would be pleasant walking around the Boeing during the external required preflight. Joe and I entered the Boeing's cockpit; I deposited my flight bag beside the left captain's seat and grabbed my flashlight. Joe sat into the FO right seat and proceeded to enter the computer's data for the flight to London. A quick climb down the external stairs off the gate had me directly under the aircraft.

I was greeted by an aircraft mechanic. "You lost, Captain?"

"No, wise ass. Never seen a captain do a walk around?"

"Shit, no, you're the first." We walked away from the exchange of words with a slight laugh and hand wave. The NY aircraft mechanics were a tough bunch of personnel at UAL and you had to earn their respect; they would not freely give it to you. I made my way to the nose gear wheel well area, and I hoped that I could remember all the checkpoints on this large 407,000 pound wide body bird.

The walk around consisted of various visual checks of critical flight safety items. This could be as easy as assuring the proper tire pressure on the attached pressure gauges on each wheel hub or the verification of safety pins removal, up lock latches, and any number of specific aircraft items deemed necessary to check per company and Boeing's specification for the Boeing 767-300. I was proud of my recalling all the areas to check, and when satisfied with my diligent safety inspection, after twenty minutes, climbed the external stairs to the gateway's entry door.

The entry door into the gateway and aircraft from the outside of the aircraft requires a specific keypad code that is randomly changed by UAL with the numbers sent to us via our company inbox. While climbing the stairs, I removed my hat to look up the number on the paper I always stashed inside my "cover." It was not there; I had neglected to obtain the new numbers, and I could not reenter the aircraft. I was mad as hell and embarrassed as this situation would elicit a great deal of teasing from all of my crew, especially Joe. This would not be good. I thought of myself as a squared away captain with attention to details. Just as I was beginning to panic, a mechanic exited from inside the door and held it open as I continued to climb the stairs. He laughed a little at me. "Forget your codes?"

I lied, "No way…just catching my breath." A quick nod of thanks and I entered the forward entrance to "1 Left" main door of the aircraft. I entered the cockpit, removed my hat and coat, while replacing my flashlight in my flight bag. I noticed Joe working on entering the various navigation and performance data through the keyboard control data unit (CDU) and with a pointing of my finger toward the cabin relayed to him that I was going to brief the cabin crewmembers on the flight information. I was greeted by the lead flight attendant (FA), "Hi, Captain Smiley. Good to see you." This nickname was for my habit of running a professional but relaxed operation by telling jokes and stories to my crew.

"Hi, Mary, how's the cabin prep going?"

We exchanged pertinent information required for the coordination between the flight and cabin crew and I asked Mary to give me a ten-minute heads-up for shutting the cabin door. I gave my normal request for a cup of black coffee, reentered the cockpit and sat in the captain's seat.

The captain's seat…the brass ring for all truly professional pilots. The coveted title of captain on a "big iron" international airline carrier, such as United Airlines, was the ultimate goal of those who aspired to reach the top of the airline pilot profession. We were the New York Yankees of the major airlines, the envy of all other airline pilots due to our worldwide international routes, our top pay contracts, benefits, and our opportunity to fly the biggest and the best—the Boeing 747-400 aircraft. I flew this 865,000 pound monster throughout the Pacific for five years and my captain's type rating on my Airline Transport Certificate always drew envious looks when I produced my certificate to captains on other airlines I was deadheading on to New York.

I gazed at the overall flight panel to see if anything jumped out at me for being out of place. I had over ten years on the various types of B-767 and the same type rating on the smaller B-757. I had over ten thousand flight hours in all their types, and I was extremely comfortable with all the various idiosyncrasies of the related types. The basic B-757 weighed 230,000 pounds and came in a variety of configurations including the ER, extended range, for international flights. The B-767 was initially designated the 200 series with a variety of configurations, but the B767-300 series was over 80,000 pounds heavier than the 200 series and was used almost exclusively for international flights. The 200 series topped 320,000 pounds whereas the 300 series topped 407,000 pounds. I flew mostly international trips and the 300 series, which I preferred as it had the feel and characteristics of my favorite Boeing, the 747-400.

The glass cockpit of the B747-400 was, at that time, the latest generation of the Boeing's computer, software, and glass instrument panel aircraft since the introduction of the B767 nearly twenty years earlier. It was PFM (pure fucking magic), the term used at UAL's training center in Denver, Colorado.

I started my cockpit flow, a term used for the initial check of displays, and ran through all the required bells and clank warning checks. I finished the checks with the required verification of Joe's programming of the FMS (flight management system) as per UAL's standard operating procedures (SOPs).

Joe was slipping back into the cockpit and asked, "Everything check okay, Skipper?" I gave a slight smirk and kiddingly remarked, "God only knows how many ways you can screw up punching the numbers. We could end up in China." He just frowned at my remark.

Mary appeared with my requested cup of coffee, and I pushed my seat back to relax for the thirty minutes that was necessary to board and "tie down" the cabin for takeoff. Joe excused himself and left the cockpit to check if there were any stunningly beautiful women waiting to be impressed by the "uniform." It brought a smile thinking of my initial introduction of the perks and benefits of being a professional pilot. These perks were quickly evaporating in today's society of always being PC.

The solitude of the cockpit allowed me to reflect on my dreaded rapidly approaching mandatory retirement age of sixty; but for now, I wanted to just sit in my seat and soak up all the sights, sounds, and smells of my "office" that was so much of my persona.

I loved my workplace, and I would greatly miss it when I had to relinquish my authority to operate my Airline Pilot Certificate due to an arbitrary age set by some bureaucrat in DC. Most of the other countries had higher ages to retire, and some had no age as long as you passed your flight physical every six months.

Joe came into the cockpit and plunked down into the right seat. Frank Bell followed him and sat in the third seat normally considered a jump seat or extra seat used for deadheading crewmembers or FAA personnel. Joe complained of the lack of any beautiful women in the cabin to impress with his macho bullshit that was required from my imagined first officer's flight manual.

I teased him, "Easy, Joe. If by some miracle you hooked up with a beautiful woman from the cabin, you would get so excited that you would probably brag to your wife."

Frank and I began to laugh; and the more Joe protested, the louder and more we laughed. Joe was getting visible annoyed at Frank, and I intervened, out of sympathy for Joe, by asking Frank if he had checked the paper flight plan geographical latitude and longitude positions against the ones in the computer's database.

Frank held up the flight plan showing the checking marks with a thumbs-up gesture.

I turned my attention to the cabin and noticed that we appeared to be almost set in the back of the bus. I placed an intercom call to Mary, and without me asking, she said, "Five more minutes, Captain."

Good, I was getting bored and anxious to get the show on the road. I gave my usual "welcome aboard" announcement and tried to dampen my Boston accent, but invariably the FA would have a remark by a passenger over how my "pawk ya caw in Havawd yawd" Boston accent was difficult to understand.

We got chimed from Mary and informed that the cabin was ready for departure. We had completed all our pre-engine start checklists, SOPs, and listened for the ground crew through the ground interconnect to come online.

"Cockpit…ground…Set for push into the inner ramp."

"Standby for push clearance."

"Kennedy ground United 996 looking for clearance into the inner alley."

"Roger…United 996…Cleared to push and start engines… Call ready to taxi."

"United 996…Roger…Will do."

"Ground…Cleared to push and start engines."

"Cockpit…Ground…Roger…Clear to start numbers one and two."

We started both engines while being pushed into position to taxi to the takeoff runway. We did our after-engine start, pretaxi checklists and called for taxi clearance. We called for ground crew to disconnect their communication attached through the wheel well area phone jacks.

"Ground…Cockpit…Roger, cleared to disconnect…Standby for a salute and release to taxi."

We got clearance from Kennedy ground control after informing that that we were ready to taxi and our clearance to runway 31L via a designated ground route was read back and verified.

After a visual observation of the UAL ground crew's salute and holding up the landing gear safety pins, to verify their removal, we began our taxi. Very aware of the close proximity to the terminal and other parked aircraft, I gentle nudged the 60,000 pound thrust turbofan jet engines to start the 407,000 pounds in motion.

As momentum increased the control steering of the aircraft became easier, but due to the size of the aircraft and height of the cockpit above the ground, it took time and skill to judge ground speed, and I often checked our generated ground speed on my instrument panel.

I started to initiate my standard taxi instructions to Joe and Frank when Joe, in his best imitation of me, rattled off my spiel: "Okay guys…Listen up…Your job is to make sure I don't get lost, cross a runway or taxiway not cleared to cross, and to make freaking sure that I don't hit a freaking thing while we taxi…Oh, I almost forgot…Make me look like I know where and WTF I'm doing and going! How's that, Skipper?"

I laughed and answered him, "You left out a few 'freakings,' but not bad."

This bantering between Joe and me caught Frank completely off guard, and he just sat indecisive to make any comment or action that the two crazy pilots may require him to take to protect the passengers and crew.

Joe did a quick reassurance to relieve Frank of any anxiety by explaining to him how I had witness a few ground accidents and knew several captains who tarnished their careers because of them.

Joe was correct; I had an inordinate amount of fear of ground-related incidents. I quickly told Frank how, as a flight engineer on a B-727, I advised a captain as we were taxing into the gate that a catering truck was too close, and we needed to stop and let him pass.

This was the captain's last retiring flight from Chicago's O'Hare's Airport, and they were having a retirement party for him in operations with his family in attendance. He waved my warning off, and he taxied the left wing into the top of the catering truck. It actually lifted the aircraft up as we crushed the top of the truck. I watched this poor soul go to pieces and lament the loss of a perfect career destroyed by one careless moment.

It left a lasting image!

We reached the "hold short" line of runway 31L, and we were advised to change to Kennedy Tower frequency. I gave the FA the last "prepare for departure" over the PA, and Joe told the tower that United 996 was ready for departure at RWY 31L.

"Roger, United 996…Taxi into position and hold."

"United 996…Position and hold RWY 31L."

I taxied onto the runway and aligned the aircraft and nose gear straight down the center line of the runway.

"United 996…Wind…300 degrees at 10 knots…Contact departure leaving 3,000 feet…Cleared for takeoff."

Last check by me: "We all set, guys?"

They both responded, "Yeah, Skipper, all set."

I slowly advanced the power levers, hesitating at the straight up position to allow the massive engines to smoothly accelerate. A check of the engine's gauges, EPR, N1, N2 fuel flow showed all normal indications.

The massive Boeing resisted the initial increase in power, but the inertia was overcome by the thrust, and we started our takeoff roll down runway 31L. The aircraft gathered speed as I controlled the direction of the aircraft through the nose gear steering and rudders through the large rudder pedals at my feet. I had my left hand on the control yoke and my right hand on the power levers poised to react to an aborted takeoff if any number of events occurred prior to our committed decision speed of V1.

Joe made the mandatory callouts, and I responded by my actions and verbal responses.

Joe called, "80 knots…thrust set…acceleration normal."

Joe called out V1, and I removed my right hand from the power levers and placed it on the yoke…We were committed to takeoff.

Joe called, "Vr…rotate," followed quickly by V2. At Vr, I pulled on the control yoke to get the nose gear to lift off the runway, and as it lifted, I relaxed the pressure to allow the aircraft to fly itself off the runway. An overzealous rotation could cause a tail strike due to the length of the 767-300 being longer than 21 feet over the 200 series.

I checked my flight instruments to see a positive rate of climb on our instantaneous vertical speed indicator, IVSI and called out, "Positive climb gear up."

Joe replied, "Roger positive climb gear up," as he simultaneously pull the gear handle to the up position. This was followed by, "Gear up… three green."

The B767 accelerated quickly as the gear retracted into their respective wheel wells and at takeoff safety altitude (TSA), lowered the nose of the aircraft and accelerated to 250 knots while we retracted the takeoff flaps on their scheduled speeds.

We were on our way to London!

A series of standard instructions, compliances, and routine climb profiles had us at 35,000 feet heading toward the northeast corner of Canada for our "drift out point" to begin our North Atlantic track (NAT), route over the north Atlantic to London.

The aircraft was on full auto flight mode, allowing the software-integrated computer system of the Boeing to fly the computer-generated flight course depicted on our displays as a magenta-colored course. Altitude and speed were controlled by the integration of the flight management computer, FMC, and the autopilot/autothrottle configuration.

PFM was in complete control, and we reverted to our system monitoring mode.

The airborne communication' ACARS printer spit out our "oceanic clearance" over the NAT route, and we settled into our en route mode of flight operations.

Frank had been doing up our "manning and sleep" schedule and asked me my preference of duty and rest. I was landing the Boeing in London and always preferred the last rest period with a wake up at least one hour before landing. It gave the best combination of rest and wake up for making a landing. This was learned over forty years ago on long thirteen-hour flights in the Navy P3 Orion.

Frank was to get the least desired first break followed by Joe… RHIP, rank has its privileges, crossed through my mind followed by a smug thought, *I've earned it.*

Frank continued to sit in the cockpit on his rest period and complained that there was no way he could sleep at such an early hour. We departed JFK at 7:00 PM or 1900 with London's time at 12:00 midnight. With a flight time about nine hours, we would normally land about 9:00 AM in London.

We got our coded knock on our cockpit door, and we let the new kid flight attendant Kelly enter the cockpit. She looked like death; a worn-out dishrag, eyes red and swollen, and a nose all stuffed up with a slight feverish ashen-colored face.

I complained, "Christ, Kelly, why are you in my cockpit? You'll infect all of us if you sneeze or cough." She gave me a pathetic look of "Please, Captain," followed by an attempt to smile and butter me up. It was comical; at my age and with her sickly appearance, there was no chance, but the sympathy route for Kelly.

I told her we would take a vote to see if she could stay in the cockpit in the spare jump seat. Joe and Frank were obviously influenced by Kelly's cute face and figure. They both answered, "Okay by me, Skipper."

They were young men and they still thought and acted through their "little heads."

I told Kelly she could stay as long as she didn't begin to sneeze or cough. She gave a slight smile and showed me her stash of tissues, nose spray, and Sudafed. A typical FA…fly when you're sick and use your sick days for days off for special life events.

Mary entered the cockpit with three first class meals for us and a crew meal for Kelly. Mary frowned at Kelly and just shook her head as she left the cockpit.

I push back my seat to place my tray in my lap and told the guys, "Okay, gentlemen… let's keep it routine and simple tonight… I'm a little beat up tonight and don't want any excitement."

We settled into a normal mixture of work and personal talk when Frank asked me where I was raised as a kid. I told him a little of my personal background and how I had flown for various corporations and an airline in the Boston area.

Joe entered the conversation with the comment that he had graduated from the aeronautical program at Northeastern University in Boston.

Joe quickly inquired, "When did you fly in the Boston area?"

I told him I flew out of the Bedford, Massachusetts, airport, and Boston's Logan airport from 1968 through 1979.

Joe asked me if I knew about the famous air rescue event that happened in the early 1970s involving the air force, coast guard, and the shutting down by the FAA Air Traffic Control (ATC) in most of the New York and New England ATC area.

I was stunned by his question.

"Where did you hear about that, Joe?"

Joe answered that it was a case study at Northeastern for the New England ASR rescue teams involving all the available components for an air rescue.

"Tell me about it."

He continued, "Some light twin pilot was flying all over New England lost in the clouds at night with no communication or navigation...I think he had a complete electrical failure and loss of one engine. They saved his ass after over three hours flying deaf and blind with all sorts of rescue attempts."

"How did they get down in one piece?"

He continued the story... "I think he followed them down through the clouds, lucky stupid bastard. Should have busted his ass. He must have been scared shitless. I know I would have been."

I answered in a serious tone, "Then you would have died that night."

Frank had a view of my face and asked, "Did you know the pilot?"

I answered, "Yeah, it was me."

"What!"

"It was me."

Joe said, "Are you serious?"

I smiled at him and said, "Yeah, kid, that was really me. They told you the wrong facts."

Frank jumped in, "Christ, Skipper...Tell us the story!"

They were all inching forward toward me and even Kelly was showing signs of life. I smiled at my young captive audience and began...

CHAPTER 4

THE STORY

November 15, 1971
Early morning

I lived in an apartment in West Somerville, Massachusetts, across the street from Tufts University where the neighborhood was a mix of single and multiple family homes wrapped around the large campus of Tufts University. A neat working class community sprinkled with more affluent middle-class homes.

I lived on the bottom floor of a home on Powder House Blvd. Road with my wife, Janet, and my two small children. My wife and I had just turned twenty-eight years of age, my daughter Michele was five years of age, and my son Andrew was four years of age.

It was a typical overcast "raw" November start to the day, and I was dressed in my old navy sweats with a wool cap as I did my morning run around the campus and town. I leaped up to the porch as I finished my run and emptied the mailbox before I entered the foyer of the home.

Janet was up making coffee, and I was surprised to see that she was up making breakfast for me since I wasn't scheduled for a flight that day. Before I could ask her, she told me that Charlie had called to tell me he needed to fly to New Jersey for the day.

I was the pilot for a company named Deckhouse out of Acton, Massachusetts, and we had a twin Piper Aztec aircraft based at

Bedford, Massachusetts, Airport. The company was a manufacturer of precut high-end homes and Charlie Califf was the company's treasurer and acted as the CFO.

I called Charlie for the details, and he informed me we needed to be at a land auction at 1:00 PM in New Jersey outside of the Teterboro, New Jersey, area.

The kitchen wall clock read 7:00 AM. I told Charlie to meet me at the Bedford Terminal at 10:00 AM and ended the conversation. I was not happy to be doing this flight as I had several personal duties to do that day. I grumbled to myself, "What good is a monthly flight schedule if it does not get followed?" I hated being on call 24-7 and yearned for the more structured life as an airline pilot. Jobs were scarce in aviation at that time, and I would have to bide my time. At least I had a flying job that supported me and my family…barely… with it supplemented by my flight instructing at Executive Flyers Aviation in Bedford.

I took a quick shower, and when I finished dressing, breakfast was on the table. My kids were up eating or rather playing with their food at the table as I sat to join them. Janet was at her permanent position at the kitchen sink washing the never-ending supply of dirty dishes. She was my high school sweetheart, and we got married at twenty-one years of age two days after I got my navy flight officer's wings and ensign commission.

Off to San Diego, California, the next day with a bundle of cash from our rather large wedding held at the rooftop of the prestigious Parker House Hotel in Back Bay, Boston. Her uncle Louie worked as the head bartender as well as the president of its union.

I was based at North Island for the Anti-Submarine School training, and we lived in Coronado Island. Somerville, Massachusetts, was a long way and a different world than California, but after my military duty tour and three squadron deployment, including two to Vietnam, we headed back home with two babies added to the family. I was discharged from the navy on November 15, 1968; today was the three-year anniversary of my discharge from the navy.

I telephoned the Boston Flight Service Station that handled flight plan filing and weather briefings; the weather was going to deteriorate throughout the day and evening with low clouds and low visibility forecasted for the entire northeast area.

I was not concerned as the twin engine PA 23-250 Piper Aztec I was flying had all the goodies. It was equipped with a full complement of radios for communications and navigation. A three axis autopilot capable of following navigation directions and a preselect altitude function. It was equipped with full deicing boots, electric heated props, and pitot tubes with a rare electric windshield deicer.

N6408Y, a 1964 Piper Aztec "C" model, was loaded and I was already a rated airline transport multiengine pilot as well as a certified FAA flight instructor on single engine, multi engine, and instrument. I had over five thousand hours of flight time and almost one thousand hours in an Aztec; I was a young, confident experienced pilot. Of course like all pilots, I was the best pilot I knew.

I teased and played with my kids for a while and as usual got them all hyped up for Janet. I didn't tell Janet what time to expect me home as I had stop telling Janet the exact time I would return from a flight because of an incident while at North Island.

I needed my four hours of required monthly flight time while in ground training at North Island in order to get my monthly flight pay, so I hopped a ride on an old sea plane P5 M used for ASW. It had old radial twin engines and the inside resembled a boat more than an aircraft. It was to be an eight-hour navigation instructing flight along the Mexican Baja Coast. I told Janet my estimate time back home, which was to be early evening.

The takeoff in the bird was rough as hell as the bow slapped against the small sea state waves; I was glad to get into the air. The noise in the back was deafening, so I opt to go to the cockpit; Jesus, what a relic!

The glow of red cockpit lights and the antique levers and switches made it appear to be a submarine. I could not believe these aircraft were still operational and actually in use in Vietnam.

After an hour, I retired to the cabin, stuff some blankets over my head to lessen the noise, and fell asleep. I awoke by a kick to my foot and the sight of the cabin door opened with the crew throwing loose equipment overboard. We had lost the right engine, and we were barely flying as we skimmed over the waves on one engine. I was hoping the goddamn rust bucket could float on the open seas.

We were now limping home on one engine. Our eight-hour flight would turn into a twelve-hour ordeal, but we finally made it back to North Island. To sit as a noncrewmember in an emergency is nerve-racking; I was exhausted and just wanted to get home.

I open the front door of our Coronado bungalow to discover my frantic wife with several officers' wives with her. She looked exhausted as she came teary-eyed toward me, and I had to stifle a laugh as she began to berate me for making her so worried and upset.

I thought, *What? It's my fault?*

I, of course, did not convey my thought to her and just held her as the wives quietly smiled and waved goodbye.

After that incident, I never gave her an exact time to land, and she never asked.

I told the kids to be good and kissed Janet goodbye. She told me not to wake her if I got home late; that was code for no sex tonight.

I laughed at her comment and left the apartment to my awaiting rusted 1964 Olds Super 88. I turned on the radio, stepped on the gas, and started out for my forty-minute ride to Bedford Airport.

CHAPTER 5

FLIGHT BEDFORD TO TETERBORO

Bedford Airport

Forty minutes later, I parked my car at the employee parking lot at Bedford and entered the civilian general aviation terminal. A quick hello to the FBO personnel in the terminal, a few friends at Executive Flyers, and I hitched a ride on a tug to Hangar number 4 where N6408Y was hangared. I was happy we had the hangar space as this allowed the aircraft to remain clear of any ice or snow and kept me out of the cold for my external preflight of the aircraft. I met up with Jim, our company aircraft mechanic who maintained our aircraft and who did all the required FAA mechanical checks. We were on a progressive maintenance scheduled that had the aircraft inspected every one hundred flight hours as well as other annual inspections or system checks.

I asked Jim if he had recharged the nitrogen charge in the "prop governors" that allowed the props to remain within a maximum range and allowed the pilot to control their pitch as required through the two prop control in the cockpit.

As usual the answer was "All set, Andy."

This charge had been mysteriously leaking, causing the props to overspeed at high power setting required for takeoff. I had aborted several takeoffs with the boss aboard, and he was not too happy over it.

I did the external and other cockpit checks while in the hangar and had them hook up the tug to the nose gear lugs to move the aircraft out of the hangar. While I was walking to board the Aztec, I noticed an object under the left wing. "Damn!" It was a dead bird! This is considered a bad omen to start a flight. Jim picked up the bird with a gloved hand and threw it in a trash barrel. He laughed at me, but he was not the one flying that day.

I promised myself not to tell Charlie about the bird as he was usually a relaxed passenger, and I wanted to keep him that way.

They unhooked the tug after pulling it out of the hangar, and I started both engines while receiving taxi clearance to the terminal. I reflected on the dead bird and laughed at my reaction...plenty of birds get trapped in a hangar and die...just an old wife's tale.

I taxied up to the terminal and shouted at the aircraft fueler while exiting the craft, "Top it off...Bring the fuel receipt inside the terminal."

Charlie was waiting for me at the terminal with a cup of coffee in one hand and his ever-present cigarette in the other hand. I asked Charlie, "What's new?"

His standard answer: "Nothing...Same shit, different day." I liked Charlie; he was a regular guy with a regular guy's attitude toward life, and he treated all with respect.

I briefed Charlie about the crap weather ahead, and it just elicited a shrug and a grunt from him. We boarded the aircraft with Charlie occupying the right copilot seat instead of going into the passenger's compartment. I think he experienced a little air sickness and sitting up front usually gave you a better ride and the visual clues kept your equilibrium in check.

The normal start and pre-departure checks were completed, and I called ground control for my filed clearance to Teterboro and taxi clearance to the active runway 29.

"Ground...Aztec 6408Y ATIS information 'A' IFR to Teterboro ready to taxi."

"Roger, Aztec 08Y...Ground...Taxi runway 29 via the outer taxiway and standby for clearance to Teterboro."

"08Y...Roger...29...via the outer."

"08 Y...Ground...Are you ready to copy clearance?"

"08Y...Affirmative...Ready to copy."

"Aztec N0648Y...You are cleared IFR to TEB as filed at 6,000 feet...Initial altitude after departure 3,000 feet...Squawk code 2634...Contact Boston departure control leaving 2,000 feet on frequency 126.5...Contact Bedford tower on 118.5 when ready for departure."

I read back the clearance as required and contacted the tower.

"Tower...08Y ready end of 29."

"Roger 08Y...Taxi into position and hold...Waiting for your clearance release."

"Roger...08Y position and hold."

I taxied the Aztec onto the runway and aligned the nose gear down the center of the runway.

"Aztec 08Y wind 260 at 10 knots...Cleared for takeoff."

"08Y...Roger, cleared for takeoff...Charlie, you all set?"

"Yeah, kid...Let's go...I need a smoke."

The adventure was about to begin...

CHAPTER 6

AIRBORNE

I gently pushed the two power levers forward and kept the aircraft on the center line with the nose gear steering and rudders through the rudder pedals. The aircraft was lightly loaded, and we accelerated quickly to a takeoff speed of about 90 knots. A quick check of the engine gauges while gently pulling back on the yoke had the Aztec leaping into the air. I always talked to myself when I was the only pilot in the cockpit to try and not forget any procedures.

I muttered, "Positive climb…Gear up."

I pull the gear lever to the up position and observed the three green up gear and lock position. Charlie held up a cigarette indicating he wanted to smoke.

I told Charlie the "smoking lamp" is lit as Charlie was beginning to get nicotine withdrawal pangs. I noticed the lift-off time and wrote it on my knee board, which I kept on the instrument panel. I never liked the damn thing wrapped around my knee because it always hit the yoke when I moved the controls.

At 2,000 feet altitude, I contacted Boston Departure control as instructed. We received our clearance to climb and maintain 6,000 feet. I set all the necessary inputs to the autopilot and pushed my seat back to monitor that the aircraft was doing as programmed.

Charlie lit his smoke and looked out as we skimmed the top of the cloud deck. He remarked how it showed the speed of the aircraft as we went in and out of the tops of the clouds. We started to pick up a trace of "Rime Ice" on the leading edge of the wings, but we were soon about 1,000 feet over the tops, and it quickly melted off the rubber deicing boots covering the wings.

I began to get a gnawing uncomfortable feeling in the back of my head that the aircraft was just not "right." I began to visual check the gauges and worked the engine controls to make sure I was getting the proper responses. Charlie saw my concern and asked me if anything was wrong.

"She just doesn't feel right."

Charlie frowned at me. "What the hell does that mean...not feel right?"

I explained to Charlie that flying an airplane is like making love to a woman. It is done by touch and pressure responses through your fingers. A pilot does not just fly with his eyes and brain, but makes love to the craft through his touch on the control yoke.

When you touch a woman, a certain response is hoped for and the same is true in flying. A touch here, a touch there, followed by a desired response. An airplane will "talk to you" through the pressures and systems in a subconscious way like a woman getting use to your touches.

This is why we call them "she" when referring to the aircraft.

Charlie laughed, but I could see he was mulling over what I said to him.

I still had that nagging feeling, but after checking everything twice just attributed it to being spooked by the dead bird under the wing.

The flight continued as planned without any glitches, and we soon found ourselves in the control of TEB approach control; I called TEB approach.

"Approach...Aztec 6408Y with you...Descending to 3,000."

"Roger 08Y... Expect visual approach to runway 06."

"Approach...we're still IFR...say TEB weather."

"Roger...TEB is reporting ceiling 1200 broken...Visibility 3 miles...Wind...050 at 6 knots."

"Roger, approach...Work us down...Will report field in sight."

"08Y...Maintain present heading...Descend to 1,000 feet... Report field in sight."

"08 Y…Field in sight."

"Roger…Contact tower on 119.5"

"Tower…08Y with you."

"Roger…08Y wind 070 at 10 knots…Cleared to land."

I began to slow the aircraft by extending the landing gear, set my landing flaps, and made a smooth touch down on runway 06 at TEB. A quick taxi had us at the ramp with engines shut down. We quickly entered the terminal to use the men's room as the morning coffee was doing its thing.

We rented a car and set out for the trip to the auction site.

CHAPTER 7

PUBLIC AUCTION

Charlie had me drive the rental as he began to read some paperwork on the proposed land to be used for some "Spec Building of Model Homes" for Deckhouse, Inc.

It was a property in foreclosure due to property tax delinquency located about an hour from the airport. I noticed the weather deteriorating and checked my watch. It was a little after noon time.

"Charlie, how long we going to be at the auction?"

"I don't know…You got some place you need to go?"

I told Charlie I noticed the conditions were conducive to freezing rain, and we wouldn't be able to takeoff if it was doing it at the airport. We would be stuck in Jersey; Charlie was not happy with me telling him that fact.

"Okay, kid…Let's hope it takes only an hour or so."

Well, that did not quite work out as we left the auction at 4:00 PM without getting the land. The trip was a total bust!

We arrived back at TEB, and the weather was down to the minimums required to keep the airport open and operational. I quickly got a weather briefing, filed the flight plan back to Bedford, and we went to the Aztec. It was beginning to drizzle, and I quickly inspected the aircraft before we both popped into the cockpit.

I started both engines, ran the checklist, and called ground for taxi and clearance to BED.

The wind was beginning to pick up and the drizzle became a steady rain. The wind created a horizontal rain shower further reducing forward visibility. That was not my concern as FAA Part 91 Operations did not restrict us on this type of weather problem. I was concerned with the freezing rain as they would close the airport.

Charlie had a concerned look on his face while holding on to the leather hand strap on the side of the door window.

"Christ, Andy...This looks scary...We good to go?"

I was about to answer him when ground control without letting me answer their initial call up rattled off our clearance and taxi instruction. This was followed by a warning I needed to get airborne quickly as they were going to be closing the airport if it got a little worse in the weather department.

I started to taxi to Runway 06 while I was reading back and confirming our flight plan clearance to BED.

"Cleared as filed...Maintain RH...Runway heading after lift-off...Initial climb to 3,000 feet expect 9,000 feet ten minutes after departure squawk 0267...Departure control frequency 126.9."

I taxied the aircraft to the holding line of 06 and called TEB tower for takeoff and release. At that time my headset jack broke, and I switched to the speaker. I told Charlie that he needed to be quiet until we got leveled at our cruising altitude so I could hear through the speaker.

Tower told me position and hold.

I complied and acknowledged the instructions.

I adjusted my seat lower than usual in order to be eye level with my instrument panel. I knew once we were moving I would have no forward visibility, and we would be in the low clouds almost immediately after takeoff. This would be a full instrument no visibility takeoff. Charlie saw my actions and became concerned.

"It looks bad out there, kid...Is this safe to go?"

I hesitated before answering. "Yeah...no problem...just need to be on my toes...Hell, that's why you pay me the big bucks."

Charlie's response was to tighten his grip on the leather strap and honker down into the plush leather seat; he looked nervous.

Tower got our release clearance and cleared us for departure.

CHAPTER 8

INTO THE ABYSS

I released the brakes and quickly moved the power lever to full power. The lightly loaded twin accelerated quickly as the down pouring sound of the rain increased with each increase in ground speed. The nose gear started to dance up and down on the landing strut as the wind changed direction and velocity causing uneven loads on the nose gear. It was difficult to maintain directional control as the wind, rain, and reduced visibility hampered the control of the aircraft. At 90-plus knots, I pulled the aircraft into the air to be met by buffeting wind shear. It was extremely rough, and Charlie was holding on for dear life. He sat deeper into his seat and cursed to himself.

We entered the clouds at about 300 feet. I retracted the landing gear while the tower told me to maintain RH, climb to 3,000 feet, started the timer from zero, "zero time" on the air craft mechanical chronometer and contact NY Departure on 126.9.

Just as I was about to contact the departure control climbing out of 1,500 feet, the aircraft swung violently to the right with the left wing rising to a dangerous angle. This was accompanied with a very loud screaming pitch sound.

Charlie screamed, "Andy, what the fuck was that?"

I knew immediately what it was—the damn prop air charge had leaked and now the prop oversped pass the red line limit. I immediately reduced the right engine to idle thrust, which brought the prop RPM down to 2,000 and preventing any overspeed damage. I continued the reduced climb to 3,000 feet and got back on runway heading.

I got a call from Departure.

"6408Y, say your heading."

"08Y...I'm coming back to 060...I have an overspeed on my right engine...Power to idle...Request level off at 3,000 feet.

"Roger 08Y...Say your intentions."

"08Y...Standby."

I needed to calm Charlie as he looked as if he was about to have a stroke. I told him we needed to return to TEB, but we were in good shape and would just leave the right engine running at idle.

"TEB...08Y...Request vectors back to TEB for approach and landing."

"08Y...TEB...You...declaring an emergency?"

"TEB...Negative...Just need to land."

"08Y...Roger...Turn left to 240 degrees for left downwind ILS 06...Maintain 3,000."

I complied with their instruction and noticed that we were accumulating ice on the wings and windshield. I put on the electric prop heaters, windshield heater, and verified that the electric pitot tube for the airspeed indicator was on. I keyed the mic to talk to approach control and noticed a dimming of the cockpit lights and an acrid electrical smell. A small flame shot out of the electrical bus bar under the instrument panel.

We had an electrical fire!

Charlie screamed to me about the fire, and I instructed him to grab a rag under the seat and grab the small fire. He complied and the fire was extinguished, but as I checked the generator power output, it indicated zero. The aircraft battery was the only source of electrical power on the aircraft. The battery normally has a life of about thirty minutes if fully charged and if the aircraft electrical drain is drastically reduced.

This was not our case as every electrical component of N6408Y was operating. The outside navigation lights, inside cockpit lights, all communication and navigation radios, and the heavy amperage load electrical deicers.

I instructed Charlie to grab my flashlights out of my flight bag. I had just purchased an additional small pen light for reading air charts at night and my large flashlight had a new set of batteries. This would be crucial to our survival that night.

I began to down load the electrical loads and at the same time declared a flight emergency to TEB.

"TEB...Aztec 6408Y is declaring an emergency...Loss of generator electrical power...On emergency battery...Right engine at idle thrust producing minimum power...three hours of fuel on board... Two souls on board!"

Charlie grabbed my elbow and as I turned to his ashen faced he screamed, "Are you fucking kidding me? How serious is this?"

Charlie had bad skin coloring due to his constant smoking, but now he looked like he belonged in a morgue.

I held up a finger to silence him and quizzed TEB.

"TEB, did you copy 6408Y's mayday?"

A weak garbled response came over the speaker.

"Roger 6408Y...Copy mayday....Maintain 3,000 feet...Fly heading 270 for approach to ILS 06...Weather at TEB...Ceiling 100 variable to 200 overcast...Visibility half mile variable to one-fourth mile...fog...rain...wind now 090 degrees at 10 knots gusting to 15...altimeter 29.89 inches...state your intentions."

State my intentions!

WTF! I just declared a *mayday*! What did he think my intentions were, fly to Miami?

"TEB, my intentions are to get our asses down in one piece!"

This actually produced a smile on Charlie's face. His coloring looked better; the initial shock was wearing off.

I asked TEB the nearest VFR weather from my position. A Mohawk aircraft who was listening to this drama chimed in that he had departed Manchester, New Hampshire, airport, and he thought we would be able to get under the cloud deck. This was another link in the chain to our survival that night.

At that exact moment it got real quiet in the cockpit. The navigational instruments showed "OFF FLAGS" and I called TEB while checking the ammeter.

No response from TEB. Zero on the ammeter.

We were now flying crippled, blind, and deaf near one of the most congested real estate areas on earth in the clouds at night. I noted the time, and my first concern was to not get anywhere near New York City.

I began a right hand turn to about 045 degrees and climbed up to my cleared altitude of 9,000 feet as filed. We were lightly loaded, and even with the reduced right engine power, it easily climbed to the altitude.

At 9,000 feet, we were in between cloud decks, and this eased my concern about aircraft icing for the moment. I instructed Charlie to grab my knee board and gave him my plan to save our asses that night.

Meanwhile, while I was struggling with our emergency, TEB was in full emergency mode.

CHAPTER 9

ZERO TIME PLUS
10 MINUTES

TEB Tower

The two FAA controllers in the TEB tower just looked stunned at each other. Supervisor Lenny D'Amato was standing behind approach controller, John Peters, seated at the radar console.

John Peters is attempting to call 6408Y.

"Aztec 6408Y, do you read TEB on this frequency? Squawk Ident if you do."

John turned in his swivel chair to Lenny.

"Lenny, we lost communications and the transponder. I got a primary target only. He looks like he swung to a northeast heading… no transponder squawk info."

"You think he lost all electrical?"

"Yeah, that'd be my guess. I heard the Mohawk pilot give the weather in New Hampshire. I don't know if the Aztec heard him."

"You have the Mohawk try talking to him?"

"Yeah, Lenny…No joy."

The two men conferred over their concern of the Aztec crashing into a city, and they hoped that the pilot at least had physical control of the aircraft. They requested area weather, and Lenny issued a notification to all FAA facilities in the area. They called all available controllers at the TRACON center as an older controller walked into the room carrying teletype weather reports. He informed Lenny that most airports between Washington and Boston were closed due to freezing rain and weather below landing minima.

John suggested to Lenny to have all airports in the entire northeast area turn their airport lights to the highest level possible as the Aztec may try to sneak under the cloud deck.

This was another link in our survival.

The entire ATC system was notified along with the Cape Cod, Massachusetts, Coast Guard helicopter ASR unit.

Our survival would depend on me not losing my head and acting impulsively. It would depend on the efforts of many on the ground and those who were about to launch and search in the sky.

It also involved a great deal of luck and it not being our time.

CHAPTER 10

ZERO TIME PLUS 15

Cockpit of N6408Y

We were in serious trouble, and we needed a plan of action. I asked Charlie to get a pad of paper and a pen from my navigation bag. Charlie tried to smile as he obeyed my order. I took out my air sectional chart and compared it with my low altitude IFR chart for distance and magnetic course from TEB to just north of BED airport along the New Hampshire border.

It was approximately 200 air miles on a direct magnetic course of about 055 degrees or a northeasterly course. We had taken off fifteen minutes earlier, but for all practical purposes with the zigzagging of our flight path, we were just northeast of TEB.

The *zero time* showed plus fifteen minutes, and I would use this watch time for our critical fuel load and our geographical position estimates.

I explained to Charlie that we were going to get to BED using a basic, *dead reckoning* method of navigation using our magnetic compass, indicated airspeed, calculated winds, and our time to figure our position along the ground.

He looked incredulously at me, but I assured him that I had used this many times in the navy on long extended thirteen-hour flights.

I kept the bad news to myself. We had no communications, no navigation; no electrical gauges worked except the self-generating engine gauges, no fuel gauges or electric fuel pumps for transferring fuel from tank to tank.

The electric flight instruments were winding down, and we were left with the engine-driven vacuum pump powered instruments along with the pitot static instruments.

We had no electric pitot heat and this instrument because of its venturi designed iced up very easily with lose of the airspeed indicator. The controls were cable, and I had a mechanical elevator trim wheel as a back up to the electric switch on the yoke. The flaps were hydraulic from an engine driven pump and the gear should free fall after it unlocked with the gear handle in down position.

I had Charlie make two columns on the paper, one for flight time and the other for time to transfer fuel. I was hoping the engine driven pumps could accomplish the transfer without the electric pumps.

I told Charlie of my plan to do time, heading, and airspeed calculations for our dead reckoning position just north of BED near Nashua Airport to try to descend under the clouds. We would be away from a city but should have enough ground lights to judge our altitude and avoid obstacles. I decided not to concern Charlie with the very dangerous chance of aircraft icing and any multitude of dangerous variables that we may face.

I saw the justified concern look on Charlie's face and tried to lighten up the situation.

With a smirk and half laugh, I grabbed Charlie around his narrow shoulders and asked him, "Hey, Charlie…Relax. Who's the best pilot you know?'

He smiled and answered, "Shit…You're the only pilot I know!"

CHAPTER 11

ZERO TIME PLUS 30

Rescue Team Members

The New York ATC, ZNY, took control of the rescue effort from TEB but would soon hand it over to Boston ATC, ZBN as our flight took us eventually into the Boston ATC sector. Boston had control of all New England at a designated altitude in various areas of traffic including a sector very near New York and New Jersey. The request went out to the Coast Guards rescue squadron at Cape Cod, which flew the large Sikorsky SH3 twin turbine helicopter.

The five crewmembers of the rescue chopper got their briefing and ran to their chopper at the ramp being prepped for flight by their ground crew. It was a very blustery raining night with the rain coming down in a deluge of sheets of water. The pilot in command (PIC) is a career Coast Guard military pilot of in his midthirties with vast experience in rescue missions.

Lt. Commander Bill Williams would need to call on all this experience and skill this night in the skies over New England. The men took their seats in the chopper, plugged into the crafts ICS intercom system and listened for the commander to have them check in over the ICS. "Okay, men, get settled in. Listen up."

The men continued to strap into their crew positions while adjusting their intercom volume. Williams got testy. "Quiet down… Listen up! We're being vectored by Boston ATC to intercept a lost twin-engine civilian aircraft near the Connecticut and Massachusetts border. The twin has no electrical power…that means he can't communicate or navigate and more important to us he will have no running lights showing. It'll be a bitch to spot him. Stay alert! Let's not run into him and screw up our beer drinking night."

Following a few laughs over the ICS, the commander relayed information on an Air Force C-130 out of London bound for DC being vectored toward the area.

"Let's not let those junior birdmen steal the show. ETA to intercept is forty minutes."

The ground crew gave the signal to start the turbines. The cockpit came alive with all the checklists and thrown switches to start the turbines. The turbine noise overcame the pelting rain noise on the aircraft and a release from the ground crew had the SH3 Chopper lifting off and quickly being swallowed by the low lying fog.

CHAPTER 12

ZERO TIME PLUS 30

Cockpit of Pacer 02

The ATC network had contacted an Air Force C-130, a four-engine turboprop cargo aircraft flying from London to the DC area. They asked for their assistance in spotting the Aztec along with the Coast Guard helicopter out of Cape Cod. The pilot in command is a mid-forties aged Career Air Force Officer Colonel Jack Winters based at Andrews Air Force Base. The colonel is listening via the long range HF radio to the rescue request from the ATC while his crew listened with him about the emergency request. The co-pilot is a young Lt. Phil Russo and the flight engineer sitting between the two pilots is NCO Sgt. Bill Walsh. They listened to the briefing and discussed the request.

Sgt. Walsh was the first to speak, " Jesus, Skipper, how the hell are we going to get a visual at night on a light twin with no running lights? We can't see two feet in front of our nose in this crap weather."

Winters just smiled at the sergeant. "We'll face that problem when we get into the area."

The colonel instructed the NCO to go back to the crew and get them into the observation window seats and connected up on the ICS for his briefing.

As he was leaving the flight deck, Lt. Russo asked, "Yeah, Skipper, how the hell are we going to get a Tallyho on that twin?"

Winters responed, "Damn if I know…If we can't find him and point him in the direction of the chopper to guide him through the clouds…well, enough said."

The colonel heard the cackle of his crewmen checking in via the ICS and observed Walsh entering the cockpit with a thumbs-up sign. The colonel briefed his crew as the aircraft changed course over the Atlantic to head toward the rescue area. The weather was now sprinkled with thunderstorms and lightning flashes, which outlined the aircraft as it flew through the sky.

CHAPTER 13

ZERO TIME PLUS 30

New York ARTCC ZNY

Lead supervisor controller, Paul Duggan, replaced the direct line phone receiver into its cradle and let out a loud whistle that immediately caught the attention of the other controllers working the midshift at ZNY, New York ARTCC.

Paul put his fingers into his mouth and an explosive whistle caught the controllers by surprise. They all turned and looked at Paul as he explained the reason for his attention getting whistle.

"Listen up…We have a potential catastrophic event developing. I need four men not working a scope to assist in this declared emergency out of TEB."

Four hands immediately shot into the air, and Paul smiled at the always enthusiastic response that a declared flight emergency mustered from the "gang" of eager volunteers.

He mentally evaluated his response team and was pleased with their experience levels. All the controllers loved the extra drama on occasion that broke up the monotonous routine of the daily grind of keeping the flow and separation of air traffic on schedule and moving safely through their control air space sector.

A senior controller named Moe asked the first question, "What's up, Paul?"

Paul explained the details of the inflight emergency relayed from TEB, and this brought forth a remark from a controller who was the shift's funny guy.

Joey, a large corpulent senior controller from Newark, New Jersey, remarked, "Christ, the twin is just trying to escape from the shit NJ stink!" This brought out a few snickers and laughs ignored by Paul. He went into more detail of the aircraft's emergency's situation.

He finished the brief and the men digested the information until controller Pete Brown just began to talk out loud.

"Paul, let me see if I got it right…This twin is flying with no electrical power…blind and deaf…added onto this is he has an engine problem"

Paul grimaced at the stark recap. "That's about it."

Pete asked him about the engine problem and if the engine was shut down. Paul informed him that the initial report by the pilot was an overspeed, but no other info was relayed to TEB.

Paul asked which controller was working the area overlap with Boston ZBN center and if he had the twin's primary target on his scope. A controller raised his hand to confirm the primary target radar return.

Controller Mark spoke for the first time by asking the question that was on all the controllers' mind by stating the obvious.

"We can't talk to the aircraft, he has no navigation guidance, and no talking to him via remote navigation VOR transceivers… How are we going to help him?"

"We have no emergency procedures that cover this situation except keeping other traffic away from the poor bastard."

Joey chimed in about the fact they could help with locating the crash site and bodies.

Paul bristled at this comment and shouted, "Everyone, shut up and listen…We'll vector rescue aircraft if he stays in our sector to assist in a visual recovery if possible."

It got very quiet in the control room as all the rescue volunteers started to digest the gravity of the rescue attempt and of the near impossible happy ending to this unfolding air drama. No professional aviation personnel accepted failure no matter a pilot, mechanic,

ATC, or any of a dozen professions that make up the "group" of the family that all men considered necessary to safely fly aircrafts.

The quiet was punctuated by the controller working the Aztec's primary radar target return of N6408Y by announcing that the airplane had entered the overlap space between New York and Boston's airspace. This statement brought a mix bag of emotions...elation of not directly going to feel the anguish of defeat, but at the same time the loss of potential glory if they pulled off the near impossible rescue. Most of the men leaned toward the odds of not succeeding and were relieved that they were not going to be directly involved in this probable tragic ending.

Paul walked over to the direct phone line between New York and Boston and as he was raising the receiver to his ear heard the familiar voice of Sal Rizzo from the other end in his obvious NYC accent declare, "We got the target completely in our sector...We'll take it from here."

Paul often wondered of Sal's connection to the city, but this was not the time to make small talk.

"Roger...You got it...Good luck, Sally."

Paul hang up the phone and looked at his men and knew they are all thinking the same thought, "They would have had a better chance to save the Aztec if they had stayed in the New York sector."

The ever-present ego in aviation is ingrained in all that serve the professional aviation community!

CHAPTER 14

ZERO TIME PLUS 40

Nashua, New Hampshire, Location of Boston ARTCC ZBN

Sal "No Neck" Rizzo absentmindedly, without looking, attempted to place the phone onto the cradle of the direct line to NY Center. The receiver missed its target and fell to the hard cement controller room floor. Sal cursed and, with a grunt, picked up the phone and replaced it in its proper place. The other controllers observed the angst in Sal's face but made no comments. Sal paused to collect his thoughts and, after getting his controllers' attention, relayed the information from NY Center.

Chris Sullivan was the first to speak, "No electrical, an inoperative engine, IFR in the soup, headed for God knows where, we can't talk to him, and he is unable to navigate. Other than those facts, we're good to go."

The "buzz" between the controllers began immediately on the best courses of action to extradite the lost twin from the clutches of a certain fatal ending.

Sal quieted their talking by banging his fist on a table.

The room immediately became quiet; Sal demanded and received instant response to the noise. He was a no-nonsense lead supervisor controller who his fellow controllers respected and feared.

The "Beast," as he was referred to behind his back, was a man that other men instantly recognized not to fuck with if they valued their health. He was all of 5 feet 8 inches tall, but weighed in at over 220 pounds of muscle and bones. This was due to his genetics that was greatly enhanced with over twenty-five years of heavy weight training as a competitive power lifter. This was his other passion besides his work at the center and his dedication to his sport resulted in a room full of trophies proudly on display at the Rizzo's home. He was forty-five years old and at the peak of his game at the center as well as a power lifter.

He waited a few seconds and reminded his crew that this would have to be a coordinated effort by ATC and the Air Search Rescue team to give the floundering and lost Aztec any chance of surviving the night.

The first order of business was to check the primary radar target returns on the Aztec; track its movements and projected track over the ground. Sal checked with John O' Brien, the controller manning the current sector that the aircraft was now occupying, and looked over his shoulder at the radar return while questioning O'Brien on the difficulty in tracking a small primary target.

He responded, "Not bad, Sal. I've lost him once or twice on a sweep, but as long as I stay focused, it should be okay provided he stays high enough in altitude."

Sal looked at the area where the light twin was tracking and became concerned with the hilly terrain under the aircraft's flight path. He mentally made a note on how he was going to coordinate the air rescue team and instructed O'Brien that he wanted him to move from sector to sector scope to track the aircraft while others manned his normal air sector.

"Okay, Sal, good with me" was the immediate reply by O'Brien.

Sal proceeded to give instruction for alerting the direction finding network, DF, and verifying the launch of the ASR chopper and the status of the Air Force C-130 flying toward the twin.

Ten minutes after the handoff from NY Center, the Boston Center was kicked into full recovery rescue mode for the Aztec boring zigzag holes in the sky.

Sal sat in his roller chair designed to move along the sectors' scopes without getting up off his ass, and this description is what Sal always used to amuse any visitors to the center. He grabbed a cup of coffee and took a five-minute break to gear up for the task ahead that evening while reflecting on his life.

Not bad for a first American generation Sicilian from the streets of NYC's The Bronx. A full-time government FAA career position with a good pay and retirement package. He had adjusted to living in Nashua, New Hampshire, and still got a kick out of explaining to people that the Boston ATC Center was actually located in southern New Hampshire. A tour of duty in the air force as a control tower operator opened the door for his acceptance into to the FAA training program where he excelled at the center of learning. His last air force tour was at the Bedford Hanscom Air Force side of the airport, and Sal was always amazed how small the world is in aviation.

He was interrupted in his thoughts by Bill Sullivan… "Sal, you want to form a distinct team for the rescue effort?"

"No" shot quickly from Sal's lips, catching Bill off guard.

"But, Sal…isn't that SOP?'

Sal barked, "Not on my shift!"

Bill just walked away knowing better to not question Sal's motive for not forming a distinct team.

Sal was upset at himself for shouting at Bill, a good guy for a "Mick" from South Boston. Sal had his reason, but he didn't want to share a piece of his personal past with his subordinates on his reason for not doing SOP procedures. The memory of that night in Germany was still fresh in his mind and was never buried deep enough to forget even after almost twenty years had passed since the incident.

He was a young air force controller on tower duty and in training as a radar approach controller for PAR/GCA instrument approaches. This is a technique where a radar display gives height and lateral displacement from a given runway and a glide path to a safe touch down.

A cargo aircraft had shut down an engine while being vectored by the initial approach radar operator and the senior training NCO on duty insisted on Sal to conduct the final PAR segment to give Sal experience under fire. Sal objected to deaf ears and all was going well until the aircraft became erratic in its altitude instructions from Sal.

This resulted in the aircraft going well below the published glide path with it disappearing from the radar presentation while disregarding Sal's instruction to immediate climb for a missed approach procedure.

The aircraft crashed not far from the end of the runway followed by a flash and violent explosion.

Sal was exonerated from any incorrect procedures, but he lived with the burden of being directly involved in the deaths of seventeen air force airmen. He tortured his mind with constant second-guessing with the notion of, "If I had corrected the sink rate just a little sooner," and he blamed the senior NCO for putting him in the position of responsibility before he felt ready for the challenge. He vowed to never have one of his controllers feel directly responsible for the deaths from any aircraft accident involving an unusual or emergency situation.

By not forming a distinct rescue team, it prevented this possibility by sharing the responsibility with all on duty to lessen the impact on any individual controller.

"Enough of the morbid memories," flashed through Sal's mind, resulting in him bolting up from his seat to face a real time emergency. He walked over to the phones connected directly to various civilian and military rescue services that would all be used before the night's flight emergency was ended. Sal requested all current updated weather reports in the Aztec's flying area and projected track area. They verified that all airports with lights were requested to turn them to full intensity, and he had his controllers scan nearby sectors to find any aircraft willing to assist them in the rescue of N6408Y.

John waved at Sal to come to the latest sector radar screen that he was using to track the Aztec. John excitedly explained to Sal that the twin was approaching the Keene, New Hampshire, mountainous area in western New Hampshire and was flying erratically as if they were looking for an airport. There was real concern that the Aztec's pilot would attempt to get below the cloud deck in an area that would surely have him hit the ground before breaking clear of the lower cloud deck.

Suddenly, controller Sam Rivers yelled across the room to Sal, "Sal, we got that military C-130 Pacer 02 on the horn. He's asking for a vector to intercept the twin."

Sal immediately left John and went to talk to the Pacer 02 aircraft.

John noticed the obvious strain on Sal's rugged face. In all other abnormal and emergency operations, he had never shown any reaction to the stress associated with an emergency situation, why was this different?

Sal and John had an almost father and son relationship even though the years of separation was less than ten. Sal seemed wiser and more experienced than any "super" his age. John was always game for the inevitable trash talk that would break out in the quiet low traffic volume time of a work shift. It would always start with a remark on the ability of a controller, but somehow terminate with an ethnic or racial background being the main contribution to the controller's superior or inferior ability to handle the air traffic.

Sal and John relished the constant combative talk of the South Boston Irish versus the Bronx Italian. Wop, Dago, Mick, Harp, Spaghetti Bender, and all reference to one's inferior heritage and bloodlines were hurled at each other, but never the word *guinea* in reference to Sal's Sicilian blood.

Guinea was off limits and woe to the poor controller in the excitement of the bantering to forget this and shout out that slur word. It did not matter if Sal was the object of the insult or if it was against another controller or just used as a reference toward Italians. The retribution by Sal for forgetting the rules of engagement and the use of the word was frightening to witness, with his physical intimidation and verbal abuse lashed out by Sal at the now cowering offender.

Sal confided in John that the word was the equivalent of calling a black man a "nigger."

"Simple as that" was Sal's dogma in keeping the word out of the control room. John knew that Sal had married a Southie Irish Lass and Sal bragged that her best room in the house was the bedroom and not the kitchen. When quizzed on his choice, his explanation was simple, but logical.

"If she's great in the sack, but a lousy cook you can always go to a nice restaurant, but if she is a great cook and no good in the sack, where are you going to go without her cutting your throat?" This always brought a smile to Sal's face.

Sal was a great kidder, but he received constant barbs on his "hobby" that required him to eat and drink the most vile producer of gas smells from his body. A constant eating of high protein shakes produced some earth-shattering release of gas that smelled so foul it caused the controllers to abandon their positions. The barbs flew when Sal farted like a cow...

"Sal, get your ass checked for damage...Sal, seek medical help for the rat that has crawled up your ass and died. And, Sal, one of these days you're going to Shit your pants."

John laughed in his head about that prediction coming true.

Sal had confessed, with the influence of too much scotch one night that during one of his explosive gas releases he felt that his shorts contained more than hot air.

He ran to the men's room, entered a stall, and to his horror had indeed shit his pants. He quickly removed his shorts, cleaned himself, and threw the shorts deep into a trash bin. He told John of the fear of being found of not having on underwear as his dick and balls were swinging freely in his pants.

He was relieved that no one discovered what had happened, and he left for home "free balling" and laughing at his stupidity of forcing the extra effort of a larger gas release.

He was in the middle of dropping his pants to put on a fresh pair of shorts when his wife walked into the bedroom and witnessed Sal with his pants around his ankles with no shorts in sight. She assumed the worse and jumped onto Sal to immediately inflict as much punishment as possible before Sal could gather his pants off his ankles. The barrage by his wife on the assumed cheating Sal produced a split lip and a right eye shiner, and it would have been more substantial if Sal had been an average man. His wife, Pat, upon finding out the truth almost joined Sal in his "short's story" by laughing so hard she had to rush to the bathroom before she wet her panties. He swore Pat to secrecy, but her promise did not extend to her family. He was a constant source of laughter as this story was retold at every family function.

John watched Sal as he started to take control of the rescue efforts, and he was elated to see a worried expression replaced with his bulldog determined face. He really loved Sal, but in the macho world of aviation no one dare to refer to another worker in this manner of expression for fear of a homophobic response by the recipient of the news.

Sal had the transceiver mic in his hand and began to rapidly relay information to Pacer 02 Air Force C-130 on the location and vitals on the light twin Aztec. The aircraft was flying from EGSS in England when it was diverted for the rescue of the Aztec.

Sal turned to John and told him to vector the Pacer 02 aircraft toward the Aztec near the Keene, New Hampshire, airport in western New Hampshire. John told Sal that the primary target was getting more difficult to track as the twin seemed to be going in circles and looked as if it was going up and down in altitude creating a no return on the radar on several sweeps.

Sal was becoming increasingly concerned on the actions of the twin and feared they may crash before the rescue aircraft reached their location.

Ten minutes after the C-130 was vectored the ASR chopper was vectored toward the twin. This greatly increased the odds of rescuing the twin aircraft.

Colonel Winters got on the ICS to brief his men on being vectored to the aircraft and to stay alert and all eyes to search the sky for the Aztec.

"I'll roger that!" came from an unknown airman over the ICS.

CHAPTER 15

ZERO TIME PLUS ONE HOUR

Cockpit of the Aztec

It was now totally dark, and it required a lot of concentration on the remaining functional flight instruments to control the aircraft. A mental inventory of the available resources available to assist in an eventually successful landing of N6408Y was most discouraging to say the least.

We had no pitot heat and the occasional flight through some clouds had me losing the proper airspeed indications. I was becoming concerned of the fuel tanks supplying fuel to the engines and of the imbalance due to the right engine being at idle and the left at a higher than normal cruise setting. We were only cruising at 140 MPH instead of our normal 200 MPH because of the reduced power, and my climb ability was also less than normal.

Charlie expressed concern of losing the engines due to no electrical power, but I explained that the engines' electrical power came off two engine-driven magnetos on both engines.

I knew as long as I kept the aircraft in gentle turns, climbs, and descents that control on partial panel would be doable in the clouds. Since we had no high RPM electrical gyro the recovery of a violent upset in the clouds that could cause a vacuum driven gyro to tumble would be difficult.

The loss of both communications and navigational capability had no standard procedure except land as soon as possible and seek visual contact with the ground.

I mulled this over in my mind. "Yeah…Good luck with that advice."

I continued to dodge clouds by varying my altitude and headings. It was becoming more difficult to return to the base heading of 055 degrees to head north of Boston. It was becoming apparent that my decision to seek an area north of Boston to let down through the clouds better be a good decision or we would not survive the night.

I continued to engage Charlie to keep him occupied by asking for a stream of headings and times on a given course, fuel times, and anything that kept him from dwelling on our dire situation. He was holding up well, considering his heavy smoking habit and not being a young man, but the stress was evident on his face.

I was hoping that my own face did not show the same doubt and fear to Charlie.

Our altitude was varying between 7,000 and 12,000 feet and our headings were erratic with attempts to avoid clouds and airframe icing conditions. The space between the cloud layers was diminishing, and I was now beginning to see flashes of lightning off in the distant cloud layers. Charlie nervously questioned me about the lightning, but I downplayed it by telling him it probably was due to static electricity from the snow showers we had begun to experience. He gave me a look. "Okay, kid, whatever you say."

I knew that a large cold front was working its way south and that could be good to clear out the scud clouds, but at the same time mixing with the relatively warm moist air could set off instability in the air masses resulting in thunderstorm activity; this would not be good!

After what seemed like hours, but was really about one hour into the flight, I decided to attempt to change the fuel tank supplying the engines. As I was about to tell Charlie, he looked at me with a pained expression on his face and asked, "Andy, do you think anybody is looking for us?"

I answered affirmative, and I explained all the rescue equipment and services available to assist the FAA in saving our asses. I downplayed the odds of them actually seeing us as it was a dark stormy night. we were a tiny unlit speck in the sky, and we had trouble staying free of the clouds. I knew our chances of our surviving this night was in my hands and on my attempt to get under the cloud deck and get ground contact. Even if we found no airport, I felt our odds of surviving a planned ditching of the Aztec with control was a lot better than running "Tanks dry" and just falling from the sky.

It was time to change fuel tanks, and I decided it made sense to try the reduced powered right engine as it was producing very little thrust because of the prop problem. The rational was that we're basically flying on the left engine, and if the fuel tank transfer did not work on the right engine, we would keep the left engine setup as configured. I did not know if the engine geared fuel pump would be able to initially suck the fuel with a tank transfer as it was SOP to turn on the unavailable electric Boost fuel pumps when transferring tanks.

Only one way to find out, do it!

"Charlie…You ready to try?"

Charlie shrugged his shoulders. "What the fuck else could go wrong?"

We held our collective breath, and we both let out a scream of delight as the right engine ran smoothly without a sputter. The real test on the left critical engine had the same encouraging results. Finally a glimmer of hope that maybe, just maybe, our luck was to change for the better.

We could not have been more wrong and right at the same time!

CHAPTER 16

ZERO TIME PLUS ONE HOUR

Boston ARTCC

As the helicopter and cargo plane were being vectored toward the Aztec, Sal became very concerned over the erratic flight pattern of the aircraft near Keene, New Hampshire. John told Sal they were trying to get the personnel at Keene to increase the airport lighting to maximum intensity, but they were unable to get anyone on the phone line.

"Shit!" Sal was furious. "What the hell was the ground personnel doing to not answer a direct line call?"

Sal made a mental note to cause as much grief to those "yahoos" as possible when he had a chance after the emergency.

Controller Sam Winston informed Sal and John that the Northeast Airlines operations in Boston just called in to tell us that they have a DC-9 departing Keene in a few minutes, and they want to relay the Aztec's position to their flight crew.

Sal yelled back to Sam, "Tell them they're circling the Keene Airport area and for their crew to keep a sharp look out because they have no running lights. Better yet, tell them to delay the departure until the Aztec clears the area."

Sam relayed the information to the airlines operation office and received an answer that they informed the captain of the situation, but that they were running late and needed to takeoff ASAP. Upon relaying this news to Sal, he stomped over to Sam and ripped the phone from his hand and shouted into its mouth piece, "Who am I talking to?"

He got a terse reply. "This is the Northeast Airline Operations on duty at Boston."

Sal took a few deep breaths to try to calm down, but the sound of his own voice soon had him *amping* up the volume. "Listen up, Mister Operations man, if I was in your shoes, I'd cancelled that flight before you're responsible for a midair collision over the Keene Airport!"

His answer to Sal only infuriated Sal beyond his control as he informed Sal that since Keene was an uncontrolled airport outside the FAA jurisdiction that until they activated their flight plan after takeoff, his authority and his opinion did not concern the airline's operations.

Sal screamed into the phone, "Asshole!"

Sal stared at the phone and slammed it onto its receiver. The control room held their collective breath as the DC-9 prepared to depart the Keene Airport.

CHAPTER 17

ZERO TIME PLUS ONE HOUR AND 10 MINUTES

Aztec Cockpit

I had calculated our position by using airspeed, time, and heading to be just about north of Boston across the state line into southern New Hampshire, but I was concerned that my east-west position was not accurate due to the constant need to change headings to avoid the clouds and of the inability to offset my headings to get back on course.

I told Charlie that we should be in the southern New Hampshire area where we heard from the Mohawk airline pilot that the base of the clouds were higher than near the coast. I told him we should be safe to at least descend to 1,500 feet in this area and that it was time to try to discover if we could get below the cloud deck. I reiterated that this was based on "our" calculations and not my calculations. This was a deliberate use of the word *our* to engage Charlie in this life-or-death decision.

Charlie looked at me and just said, "Okay, Skipper."

He was beginning to call me Skipper instead of his usually calling me kid or Andy. I assumed that this was to bolster his confidence in me and the term *kid* did not convey that confidence.

The plan was to initially descend to 3,500 feet, and if no ground contact at that altitude after five minutes to descend another 500 feet and repeat the process while trying to fly a grid type pattern that I had used in the Navy's P3 Patrol aircraft searching for downed pilots in the waters off Vietnam. We were to repeat the process until we got to 1,500 feet. It all sounded very reassuring to Charlie that I had been in Nam and familiar with the procedure, and he seemed more relaxed than he had a right to be as N6408Y slipped into the dark murky fall clouds seeking a path out of this deadly game.

I instructed Charlie to mute the bright flashlight beam by placing the rag over its lens to protect my night vision and the reflected glare of the windshield.

We entered the clouds at 9,000 feet in a slow as possible airspeed and a rate of descent of 200–300 feet per minute while maintaining a shallow 15 degrees of bank to the right. I asked Charlie to note the time and to remain very quiet as we descended lower into the thicker cloud deck.

I strained my eyes as if I could see through the dark clouds and carefully nursed the Aztec into the unknown autumn sky.

At around 5,000 feet, I started to feel a slight vibration from turbulence through the control yoke as an indication that we were entering an area of disturbed air. The weather conditions, wind, cloud type, and temperature did not support the formation of turbulence especially at night, and it quickly registered in my head that this type of uplift in these conditions was probably due to winds blowing over high terrain or hills.

I took immediate action and powered up the left engine to begin a climb while pushing the right engine as much as I could and still keeping it from overspeeding.

At about 6,500, feet we broke out between cloud decks and to my horror we saw an airline jet climbing through the lower cloud deck on a collision course with us. We were so close we could see the pilots looking out their cockpit windows searching the sky presumably to avoid hitting us. I rolled the Aztec rapidly to the right and told Charlie to hit him with the flashlight beam. The light reflected off their circuit breaker panel in their cockpit behind the captain, but before we could determine if they saw us, the Aztec got caught in the jet's vortex and rolled violently to the right, resulting in the aircraft to become inverted as we reentered the lower cloud deck at 6,000 feet.

We had been hit by his "wake" turbulence due to our close separation of no more than 50 to 75 feet in altitude and only a few feet horizontally.

I was too low to try to "Split S" out of the inverted flight and the gyros were unreliable, as the rapid displacement had them hitting their gimbals. I quickly continued the roll to the right and prayed that I got some sort of visual clues to the aircraft's attitude. I had brought both engine power controls to idle, watched my airspeed as a secondary indication of my nose attitude while watching my vertical speed and altimeter to determine my rate of descent. Suddenly there was a giant vibration and shuttering of the aircraft and at first I thought we may have sustained airframe damage from contacting the jet. I had my right hand on the power levers and felt the vibration in my hand. I told Charlie to flash the light onto the engine gauges and saw the source of the vibration as I got a glimpse of open sky and brought the aircraft to a level and upright position.

The right prop governor had freed itself with the high load on it and the prop position was brought back by me into almost the feathered position thus causing the severely reduced prop RPM and the vibration. I slowly pushed both prop controls to an even cruise position and increased my power levers to climb to a higher altitude. I leveled off in between cloud decks at 9,500 feet and started to hoot and holler, "This is fucking great!"

Charlie screamed at me, "What's so fucking great? I almost shit my pants, banged my damn head on the ceiling, and I feel like I'm having a heart attack!"

I started to laugh so hard that he must have thought I had gone crazy.

I explained to Charlie that I knew where we were in New Hampshire, that we now had full power back, more options, and a more defined plan to get out of this nightmare.

Charlie lit a cigarette and asked me to please explain what I was raging about to be such good news.

I asked Charlie to light me a smoke.

Charlie replied while lighting one for me, "Okay, but you don't smoke, do you?"

"What…I'm afraid of dying from lung cancer?"

I took a drag from the smoke, and I marveled how good it was after all those years of not smoking. It must be because I'm so glad to be still alive.

I told Charlie to listen up. "Okay, Charlie, here's the news and the plan."

CHAPTER 18

ZERO TIME PLUS ONE HOUR AND TWENTY MINUTES

Boston ARTCC Control Room

The controllers collectively held their breaths as the Northeast Airline DC-9 departed Keene Airport without causing a nightmare midair collision. Sam had reported that the Pacer 02 cargo plane had reported on station near the Keene Airport a few minutes before the DC-9 had departed the airport.

Suddenly the Pacer 02, over the control room speakers, excitedly reported seeing the Aztec as it had entered another cloud deck near Keene. The Aztec gave no sign of having seen the air force plane.

The ASR chopper was now in the vicinity of the sighting of the Aztec by the cargo plane and began a search pattern to find the Aztec. Both aircrafts were receiving radar vectors by the controllers to intercept the Aztec.

The chopper crew was encouraged from the news of the sighting of 08Y by the Pacer 02 C-130 even without a response from the twin's pilot of any indication that he had seen the large cargo aircraft. The en route flight from Cape Cod by the chopper had all the drama of a staged commercial radio broadcast as the chopper crew had a continuous monitoring of the radio frequencies used by the ground and flight in their rescue efforts.

The chatter of the rescue target area was intensifying as the cargo plane reported getting closer and closer to the Aztec and the C-130 turned on their landing lights, which illuminated the clouds.

CHAPTER 19

Zero Time Plus
Ninety Minutes

Cockpit of Aztec

Charlie took a long drag on his smoke and blew the smoke slowly and deliberately through his nose and mouth. He had a quiet pensive look on his face, and he stared at me a few moments before speaking.

"Okay, Skipper. What's this grand plan of yours going to be?"

I explained to him that we had been circling over Keene, New Hampshire, airport when we had encountered the Northeast Airline DC-9 taking off.

Charlie took another drag. "I'm not even going to ask how you know all that information, but how do you know?"

I kidded Charlie on my superior intellect and then explained it to him.

"Everybody knows that the only airport outside of Manchester operating DC-9's is Keene and that the only airline operating DC-9's in this area is Northeast Airlines."

Charlie laughed and informed me that maybe in my world everyone knew what I just told him, but not in his world.

He looked at me. "Okay, smart-ass, how does that info help us to get the Christ on the ground in one piece?"

I explained to him that our estimate of traveling north was accurate, but that we had traveled too far west of the area we had intended to be near. Keene was about due west of Manchester, and we needed to travel east on a compass heading of 090 degrees.

We were now cruising at about 170 mph as I kept the power slightly back from normal cruise to help me avoid the now thicker clouds forming in the area. We were now seeing more lightning in the clouds and entering areas of snow showers, which caused the windshield of the Aztec to give off the eerie glow of static electricity known to seamen as St. Elmo's fire when it was evident along the large mast poles of ships.

I did some navigation computations and handed the paper to Charlie while giving him a brief update on why my confidence had increased on getting us out of this nightmare. First of all, you need to know where you are located to get to another destination, and we knew we were over the Keene Airport. We knew the distance and course to our desired destination, and it now was just basic navigation of time, speed, and heading.

One other factor was we now had full power available, which gave us the option of trying to climb on top of all the cloud layers to see if we could spot an open area to let down through the clouds.

My confidence seemed to comfort Charlie, and he sat back on his seat more relaxed. I didn't bring up the fact that our fuel calculations had gone to shit and that I had not been able to adjust for the different power settings of the engines to calculate the amount of fuel in each tank. With a little luck, the current tank to engine fuel supply would work until we landed.

We were zigzagging around some clouds at about 9,000 feet when out of nowhere a mass of lights and whirling blades appeared directly in our path. I chopped the power to idle and rolled hard left to a wing's vertical position to avoid hitting what I knew had to be a large rescue helicopter.

On cue…"Andy, what the fuck was that?"

Without hesitation, I answered Charlie.

"That, Charlie, was one big mother of a chopper we almost hit. It was big…had to be a rescue chopper…probably a Sikorsky SH3 ASR from MA."

Charlie look incredulously at me before he quipped. "Yeah right…What's the pilot's name?"

I explained how that they must be looking for us because ATC would most certainly keep aircraft clear of our area and that the SH3 was a common helicopter used by the Coast Guard for air sea rescue.

I circled back to try to relocate the chopper, but we could not find him as the cloud coverage was getting thicker as we flew more to the east.

A few moments later, we spotted the most beautiful sight in the night's sky. It was the cargo/transport aircraft circling at our altitude of about 8,000 feet between cloud layers. I recognized the four-engine turbo prop as a C-130 and that he must be part of the search and rescue effort for us. I told Charlie to flash a series of off and on with the flashlight pointed at him as I maneuvered the Aztec closer to the cargo plane.

The cargo aircraft responded by flashing its landing lights off then on while Charlie, overcome with emotion, began to grab my face with both his hands and kiss my cheeks as he yelled, "They see us! They see us!"

The aircraft again gave the landing light signal as an indication of us to follow him.

I informed Charlie of what they wanted us to do, but I was concerned that because of the visibility and thickening of the clouds that I may get too close for comfort.

My fears were soon to materialize into reality.

CHAPTER 20

Zero Time Plus One Hour and Forty Minutes

Boston ARTCC

The flight deck of the cargo aircraft quickly told Boston ATC of the encounter with the Aztec. His crew began to shout over the ICS with excitement over finding the twin, and Winters had to remind them that the mission was to get the Aztec safely on the ground, not just locate him. They told Boston that they had made fifty-one passes on radar vectors from them and utilizing their own airborne radar before they started to vary the altitude on each run at the twin. Our clearance by ATC was to cruise at 9,000 feet and normally that is the altitude that you would maintain, but the rule book was thrown out in our case as it did not conform to any emergency contingent by the FAA rule book.

Winters expressed a little more optimism to the controllers on being able to get the Aztec safely onto a runway.

The news in the control room had the same effect as on the cargo plane, and Sal told his controllers to calm down as the most difficult part of the rescue was just beginning for the Aztec.

Sal knew that it had been almost two hours since the Aztec had declared its emergency, and he knew time and fuel were getting critical for a rescue.

Sal stood behind the row of controllers and spoke, "Okay, listen up! We're getting fuel critical on our rescue mission. If we fail to get that twin to follow one of the rescue planes ASAP, he's going to go tanks dry according to his original FOB on his mayday."

Sam butted into the conversation by stating that the pilot must know how much fuel he has remaining and asked, "What do you think he will do?" The room got very quiet while the controllers pondered their educated guess based on their experience and gut feelings.

John threw in that the pilot may not exactly know much fuel he has left as the fuel gauges are electric and that they had to assume they were not working for him.

"Shit..."

John further stated, "There is no way we can know what that pilot is thinking or what he's planning to do, if anything, based on the circumstances. This is the first time for me, and I assume you guys that we've handled a loss of communications, navigation, and a mechanical failure at night in complete shit weather. Throw in icing conditions beginning to form to put icing on the cake. I just hope the pilot can hold it together and not panic."

Sal reminded everyone that the pilot didn't seem to be panicking but rather doing the only thing possible to try and find a way to go visual flight conditions.

Bill came across the room holding a teletype message in his hand with information on the aircraft registration and the pilot.

He handed the paper to Sal without saying anything, and Sal took the paper without questioning its details. Sal reads the information and question Bill on how they got it.

Bill answered, "Most came off the on-file flight plan, but we called the Bedford Tower. They know pretty much who flies out of their airport. They knew it was corporate owned. They suggested we try the Executive Flyers Flight School on base since they probably knew the pilot."

Sal relayed the information to his controllers. "Okay, guys, we have some info on our aircraft and pilot. The aircraft is owned by a Corporation called Deckhouse based at Bed. The pilot is named Andy Angelo. He's a Vietnam vet that had some training at Executive Flyers a few years back after getting out of the navy to get his FAA Instructor Certificates.

"He's been flying for Deckhouse a few years, and he also does some part-time contract instructing at the flight school for advanced flight students. He's young, but experienced. They know the guy with him is an executive at Deckhouse, but no one is answering the phone at their office so we don't know who he is at this time."

Sal asked if they knew any personal information on the pilot that could help in the rescue. Bill informed him that the pilot is in his twenties, and they knew he was married at the school as he brought his son and daughter with him when he visited the flight school. Bill also relayed that he topped off his tanks at Bedford, but not at TEB.

The men looked at each other when this information registered on just how critical the fuel remaining was going to hamper their rescue attempts. By the time they got him in position at Manchester Airport to hopefully follow the chopper down to a landing, he'd be about bingo fuel or dry tanks.

Sal walked over to Bill and placed his hand on Bill's shoulder with a slight squeeze. This was Sal's way of apologizing for his outburst at Bill when he asked Sal about forming a distinct rescue team. Sal had great difficulty in verbalizing any manner of an apology, but Bill recognized that this was Sal's method and nodded his head while smiling at Sal.

Sal reread the information and thought to himself, *Angelo...a Paisano...not much older than my own son...Hang in there, kid.*

A personal connection had been made to the pilot and increased Sal's resolve and efforts to rescue the aircraft, but it would deepen the despair if they failed in their rescue attempt.

CHAPTER 21

ZERO TIME PLUS
TWO HOURS

Cockpit of N6408Y

As I began to follow the cargo aircraft, I had to get closer and closer to him as the clouds were getting thicker, and we had snow showers in the area. I was more than a little concerned on how difficult it would be to follow the large turbo prop due to the wake Turbulence and prop wash if we got too close to the aircraft. I did not want to tease the animals again and have a repeat of the DC-9 incident.

I informed Charlie that we would have to stay close and slightly above the cargo plane to keep him in sight and to avoid the turbulence that he created with his props and wing tips. The turbulence flows behind the aircraft, but quickly drops down from its flight path provided it is not redirected by any obstacle. We were in the air clear of any such obstacles and the wind did not seem to be a factor.

I pushed the power to max cruise in order to try to keep up with the C-130 who was far below his normal cruise speed. I checked our heading, it was 090 degrees, and it encouraged me that I had figured correctly from the incident at Keene. I told Charlie that I was going to position us slightly above and to the left of the air force plane and that I wanted him to zero in on its rotating red tail light to instruct me on our position with him. We were getting in and out of clouds, and I needed to keep us flying level by occasionally checking the cockpit flight instruments; I needed an extra pair of eyeballs looking outside.

We were following the aircraft on the 090 degrees heading for about five minutes when the clouds thickened, and I dropped too close to the plane, causing a violent roll to the left followed by one to the right. I quickly added full power and climb higher into the cloud deck to escape the dangerous turbulence.

As we climbed above the C-130, we reentered the cloud deck at about 9,000 feet and did not exit them until nearly 11,000 feet. We had picked up some rime ice on our windshield and wings' edges. I thought, *Just something else to worry about this night.*

I was almost in a panic mode not knowing our real fuel situation when I made the decision that I had enough information on where we were located and enough knowledge of the southern New Hampshire area to make our survival plans based on our actions and to not try to follow the C-130 any longer. I estimated that we would be in position near Manchester Airport in about thirty minutes at our current airspeed.

I told Charlie that I wanted to try to climb on top of all the clouds to see if we could spot any clear areas or bright lights through the clouds indicating a city below the cloud deck.

I asked Charlie to sit back in his seat and not smoke and informed him that we may have to get high enough that he may feel the effects of the altitude.

I kidded him not to worry or get too anxious if he got dizzy or confused as I would not kill him from the lack of oxygen.

He gave me a grunt and a "Gee thanks."

We started our climb with full power at 12,000 feet.

CHAPTER 22

ZERO TIME PLUS TWO HOURS AND TWENTY MINUTES

Boston ARTCC

There was some good news from the ASR chopper as they reported that they had a visual on the Pacer aircraft as well as the Aztec. The two rescue aircraft communicated over the best course of action to get the Aztec to follow them to the Manchester Airport area.

The Aztec's low fuel situation and the difficulty of staying free of the clouds while the Aztec was following the C-130 plus the difficult task of how to best set up for the Aztec to follow the chopper down under the lower cloud deck was discussed by both crews.

Just as the two aircraft were pondering the best course of action a voice from Boston ARTCC boomed over their headsets.

"Rescue Pacer 02...Coast Guard ASR...This is Senior Controller Sal Rizzo at Boston Center...Let me know when you are ready to copy some updated area and Manchester Airport weather."

The weather was relayed to the flight crews and the three rescue elements of the Boston ATC, the Air Force C-130 Pacer 02, and the Coast Guard ASR chopper discussed the pros and cons of having N6408Y try to let down through the cloud following the ASR chopper in such close proximity to the city, but they decided that the ceiling height and visibility were good enough to allow a safe descent by the Aztec.

Sal had John issue radar vectors to the Chopper and Pacer 02 to Manchester Airport, KMHT, and both confirmed that the Aztec appeared to be trying to follow the Pacer aircraft. While flying toward KMHT, it became impossible to remain free from the enveloping clouds and both Pacer 02 and the ASR chopper voiced their concern to Boston Center.

Sal heard the news and asked John if he thought the twin was still following the rescue planes.

John answered, "It appears he is, but I can't know if he has a visual on them or just flying his last heading."

Sal was beginning to second-guess the decision to have the Aztec follow the Pacer and Chopper aircrafts to the KMHT airport. The doubt that the light twin could maintain a visual contact with either rescue planes caused a slight panic in the pit of Sal's gut. He had to make a strong effort to quiet the fear rising through his body in order to make sharp decisive decisions. Sal was not used to feeling this amount of anxiety over any other emergency that had occurred in his work at the center.

He took a deep breath and quietly confided in John his fear of making the wrong decision to proceed to KMHT because of the very real chance of the twin experiencing fuel starvation and having an uncontrolled descent into the surrounding city. John quickly tried to relieve Sal's anxiety by offering that the only chance for a survival of N6408Y was the course being followed and the one that all involved in the rescue had agreed upon.

"It's out of our hands, Sal…We need a little help from the man up there and a shit load of luck to pull this off."

Sal smiled at John for his effort to lessen his burden, but he knew that he had made the ultimate final decision and that he would bear the consequence of it for the rest of his life. This was different than in Germany those many years ago. Then he could hide behind the decisions and actions of the NCO in charge, but here he was in control and had made the final decision.

In the cockpit of the C-130, Col. Winters was intently trying to fly the C-130 as slow as possible to try to match the much slower cruise speed of the Aztec. He was "flying on the props," an old pilot's saying that meant they were flying as slow as possible. It referred to an aircraft flying with a reduced air flow and lift over the aircrafts wings and literally using the power of the engines to raise the pitch of the aircraft into a slow flight condition.

The cargo aircraft was flying at about 220 knots, but Winters didn't know if this was slow enough for the Aztec to keep up with them. He hoped that the chopper could hover back and keep a visual on the twin. The time of getting in position near KMHT seemed to drag on forever and then...

The ASR chopper reported that he had lost sight of the twin and that they appeared to have climb back into the higher cloud deck. The chopper was scanning in all directions but reported negative contact on the twin to the Pacer 02 and Boston ATC.

Sal bolted to John's position and was almost afraid to ask if he was still getting a primary target return on the Aztec. Sal pointed to the radar scope. "Is that him?"

John answered, "I think so, but he is falling off on his course to KMHT."

Sal's imagination got the better of him, and he had the thoughts of a disaster happening on his watch.

"Please don't let this happen," screamed in his head, "not after what that poor pilot and passenger have already gone through this night. Give us a break...anything...Don't let them die after all this!"

Sal felt a wave of total exhaustion wash over him, and he tried to imagine the emotions and drama of the pilot and occupant of N6408Y.

He started a mantra in his head, "I will not let this plane crash...I will not let this plane crash!"

Williams was yelling at his chopper crew to stay alert. "Find that twin again." He knew their odds of survival were quickly diminishing with each passing minute. This could turn into a real cluster fuck if they didn't reestablish a visual on the twin, and he wanders down through the clouds on his own.

The three men—Winters, Williams, and Sal—men of unquestionable skill and courage in their professional aviation careers were facing fear for the safety of the Aztec and the doubt on their course of action now in play.

The three sat in silence pondering the fate of N6408Y!

CHAPTER 23

ZERO TIME PLUS TWO HOURS AND THIRTY-FIVE MINUTES

Cockpit of N6408Y

I began the attempt to climb over the top of all the clouds at 12,000 feet. I was maintaining a heading of due east, 090 degrees on the compass directional gyro and kept my pitch shallower than a normal climb hoping to reduce any icing on the underpart of the wings. With full forward props and the power pushed to maximum this gave us an initial rate of climb about 500 feet per minute. The aircraft was rated for a maximum of 5,300 pounds; with just Charlie and me aboard with minimum fuel, we were well under this weight. I figured that without icing, we could top 20,000 feet in altitude and prayed that it would give us a clear view of a distant horizon and some possible city lights.

We entered a more solid cloud deck at 15,000 feet and noticed that I had lost my airspeed indicator due to its pitot tube icing up. I had on the alternate, inside cabin, static ports selected so I was not concerned about losing the altimeter or the vertical speed indicator (VSI) as we continued our climb. We started to see lightning, and we entered an area of a large updraft that aided our climbing efforts.

This was a good thing, but it could be an indication along with the lightning that a rare cold air thunderstorm was brewing directly under our aircraft.

The vacuum pump driven artificial horizon had settled down, and it was giving accurate pitch and wing's angles indications, which I now had to totally rely on as an indication of desired climb airspeed. As we ascended into the higher altitudes, Charlie became very quiet and was sitting deep into his seat while holding on to the side leather strap.

I moved my seat forward and, as I did, noticed for the first time that my feet were almost frozen from keeping them constantly on the rudder pedals. We had no cabin heat as it ran off of a "Janitrol cabin heater," which was basically a burner can utilizing the fuel from a separate feed with a "glow plug." This operated electrically and had an automatic shut off feature if it lost its power.

I pulled my feet a little off the rudder pedals to cut down the cold air that was hitting my feet through the forward baggage compartment; it helped very little.

The higher we climb, the faster the airframe and prop ice accumulated. We heard a *whack, whack* banging the side of the aircraft, which startled Charlie from his almost comatose state.

Charlie grabbed my right arm. "Andy…what's that?"

He left out the "fuck."

I explained to him not to worry as it was just the ice accumulating on the props and being thrown off as it accumulated and hitting the side of the aircraft.

This seemed to calm him down as he again entered into his protective cocoon.

I neglected to tell him that the ice on the prop also degraded the ability of them to produce the much needed thrust we needed for the climb to get on top.

At this point, I became very angry with the entire situation and screamed into my head, "Fuck you both, God and the devil, neither one of you are getting our souls tonight!"

I laughed to myself as it actually amused me after I had the thought cross mind, but I was determined to not let this be our last night alive. I asked Charlie how he was holding up, and he gave me a weak smile with a thumbs-up indication.

I was concerned for Charlie since he was a heavy smoker and probably around fifty years of age, but the attempt to climb on top was deemed necessary by me. I also noticed that I was beginning to feel a little light-headed as we passed 18,000 feet. I had stopped smoking while in Vietnam due to my fear of having to run through the jungle to avoid capture if we had to bail out over enemy territory. I was always physically active, and I had an exercise program since I was just a little kid of eleven years old. I busted my ass working in the summer, as a teenager, mixing and carrying buckets of cement up and down stairs with my father's tile installation company.

I was only twenty-eight years old and ran about thirty-five miles a week; I thought, *Twenty-three thousand feet...piece of cake.*

I really had to milk the altitude as we passed through 20,000 feet to keep the bird climbing. The clouds were beginning to thin, but we were still accumulating structural ice.

I began to talk out loud to the aircraft as it clawed its way to the higher altitudes.

"Come on, sweetheart...You can do it...A little higher, baby."

The next couple of minutes are still a cause of confusion in my mind as I try to make sense of what happened next in the climb.

I seemed to be completely aware of my actions and surroundings when all of a sudden I heard my father's booming voice yelling at me as he did when he woke me up at 5:00 AM to get up for work.

He used my family name that my wife, family, and childhood friends still called me.

"Butch... Butch...Wake up!"

It shocked me, and to my surprise it was if I had passed out due to the altitude. All I know is that a few seconds later, I looked at the altimeter as it read 23,000 feet. We were on top with fingerlike wispy streaks of clouds stretching out to reach higher into the black star-filled sky above us.

I quickly checked the heading of 090 degrees and saw the beautiful sight of a large glow underneath a cloud deck off in the distant horizon. My euphoria was about to turn into a horrific ride into the bowels of a developing ascending cumulus cloud.

The aircraft aerodynamically stalled as the altitude and ice accumulation completely exhausted its lift capability. I instinctively let the nose fall while keeping wings level, chopped the power, and our initial descent was fairly smooth. I checked over at Charlie as he now was sitting with his eyes closed and breathing at a rapid rate.

The altimeter and the VSI showed a rapid rate of descent, and as my control over the stall allowed me to check its rate, I gently pulled the aircraft's nose up. We were suddenly in warmer air rising from lower altitudes as a result of the building of the towering clouds, which had the good effect of shedding the ice accumulation, but also had us entering areas of violent turbulence.

We began to get slammed around and jolted as we got caught in the rising air and now heavy rain and sleet. The noise from the sleet was deafening, and I had to struggle to keep the aircraft under control as we kept descending. We were getting tossed in our seats against our seat belts as Charlie and I had our heads slam up into the ceiling and against the side windows. We were taking a beating along with the Aztec, caught in violent up drafts and down drafts created by the cumulus cloud developing into a more violent cumulus nimbus thunderstorm. In violent turbulence it is paramount to try to keep wings level and your attitude under control to prevent a structural over load of the aircraft's airframe and the ultimate failure of a wing causing an uncontrolled flight and certain death.

I glanced at Charlie, but he showed no signs of opening his eyes while he kept a death grip onto that leather strap.

We finally spit out the bottomed out of the cloud at around 7,000 feet, and I quickly headed for a clearing between the clouds directly on our course heading.

Charlie was beginning to stir in his seat as he sat upright and with shaking hands lit a smoke. He gave me a "WTF" look, but did not say it.

I laughed and kidded him on that was not too bad.

He exploded, "What the fuck! Are you kidding me? Jesus, Mary, and Joseph...I can't take much more...just push the fucking aircraft into the fucking ground...Let's end it now!"

I just looked at him, and we both burst out laughing. He quickly grabbed my arm. "I'm only kidding, kid."

We laughed harder.

"Don't worry, Charlie...Nobody's dying on my watch."

He handed me a lit smoke, and we sat back puffing away as we knew we had just cheated death in this round.

CHAPTER 24

ZERO TIME PLUS TWO HOURS AND FORTY-FIVE MINUTES

ARTCC, ASR, PACER 02

Sal hovered over John's shoulder staring at the radar display trying to separate the primary target return from the ground clutter of the hills. He pointed his finger at the small white blue dot on the screen and gave John a facial expression of asking a question.

"Yeah, Sal, that's him, but his return is weaker."

Sal asked with a tension and a sound of despair in his voice to no one in particular. "have all the local airports been notified about max lighting intensity?"

Bill was surprised at his question as that was one of the first things that they did at the beginning of the rescue drama. He answered in the affirmative to Sal as he walked over to him.

He spoke very softly in a whisper to Sal. "Sal, you need to stay calm. show no emotion. The guys are showing signs of strain due to the constant tension and unknown outcome."

The statement caught Sal off guard and for a brief moment caused anger to be reflected in his face as a red blush, but he quickly regained control of his emotions and gave Bill a nod of thanks.

Colonel Winters was growing more anxious with each passing moment of "negative contact" reported by his observers at their stations. He knew the odds of a successful recovery were rapidly evaporating with each passing second as they scan the skies for N6408Y.

He cursed to himself, "Where are you? You little fucker, where are you?"

Tiredness was weighing heavily on Winters's brain and body as he had to constantly shift his weight in his PIC seat to stay alert. He bemoaned his aging body to his copilot and recalled earlier longer emergency rescue where fatigue was never a factor though the flight time was much longer.

Constant exercise, conditioning programs, proper diet, and all attempts to delay the aging process was no substitute for youth and its benefits to its owner.

Commander Williams strained against his seat belt restraints as he tried to pivot his view in all directions to search for the Aztec. The chopper crew was frantic in their search as they were the only real rescue craft on site. This burden was more oriented as a duty and not an assist to the FAA. Their primary mission as a Coast Guard ASR craft was what the letters on the side of the chopper indicated, air sea rescue.

Williams began to talk in his head, "Christ, where the hell did you go? He couldn't have gone far" ran through his mind.

No visual sighting, no rescue possible. This hard, cold fact weighed heavily on the commander.

The Boston Center room was void of any extraneous voices not connected to the rescue attempt and the normal communications to other aircraft in different sectors, when necessary, was subdued so as not to disturb the rescue controllers. The tension was increasing with each passing moment the Aztec remained hidden from the eyes of the rescuers. The controllers let out a constant stream of blowing air and sighing sounds of frustration on their negative rescue results.

Sal paced the floor as a waiting expectant father; back and forth, up and down, sitting, standing and a constant changing of his location among the controllers to lessen his tense body and calm his nerves.

This "dancing" caused the other controllers to reflect on the dire circumstances unfolding beyond their control, and it was reflected by the increasing pungent body odor from the nervous controllers mixed with the heavy layer of cigarette smoke.

A stepped on transmission from the chopper and C-130 from a simultaneous keying of their transmission signals caused a garble but readable…"This is Pacer 02…We see him …We see the Aztec! He's due west of our position…lower above the cloud deck."

Sal grabbed the transmitter mic and screamed, "Does he see you? Does he see you?"

CHAPTER 25

ZERO TIME PLUS THREE HOURS

N6408Y

We maintained a heading of due east as we were approaching our point to attempt a descent down to treetop level if necessary to get under the clouds. Hopefully, we would get some ground contact to at least allow a controlled crash landing. I had to vary our altitude to stay clear of the clouds, but I noticed that the clouds were beginning to get thinner at our altitude the farther we headed east toward the KMHT Airport.

I started to brief Charlie on the procedure I was going to use in our final desperate attempt to get visual contact on the ground. He listened to me, but I could see that his mind was wandering on personal thoughts and the possibility that we could both die this evening.

I tried to reassure him that no matter what happened during the descent that the aircraft would be configured and flown so as to minimize a crash landing into the woods of New Hampshire.

"Don't worry, Charlie, nobody is dying tonight. This bird is built like a tank. We'll be slow enough with minimum sink rate to survive a crash landing."

Charlie tried to smile as he responded to me. "WTF...sounds good to me."

We were about ten minutes to my estimated location of being due west of the city of Manchester, New Hampshire, just north of the city of Nashua, New Hampshire. The town had a general aviation airport with night lighting and a good 5,000 foot runway. The airport was away from the city, but I was hoping that the city lights would show us the way to the airport or to a good location to ditch the aircraft while we still had fuel enough for a powered, control descent.

The minutes ticked by very slowly and in this brief respite from activity my mind wandered to my wife and family. My wife was strong, but not that strong; we had grown up together as kids and dated through high school, my college years, and my naval flight training years. She had endured the worry of my combat flying in Vietnam in addition to the upset and constant moving while I was on active duty in the navy.

We had been separated more than being together while in the navy, but we still manage to have two kids a year apart.

We had just settled into my post-military career, hoping for that elusive airline job while my income from the jobs available barely covered our living expenses.

My daughter, Michele, was five years of age and very bright for her age. The concept of death and its meaning would be very clear to her, causing her a very emotional upset. My son, Andrew, was four years old and a very different personality than Michele. He was like Howdy Doody; a real boy who clung to his mother. He was timid but very bright in every aspect in his curiosity and attempts at new adventures.

These thoughts had to be pushed from my mind to not cloud my thinking on my actions ahead that would determine if Charlie and I would ever again see our families. I had promised Charlie that we would be okay and survive this dangerous nightmare while my own words to him comforted me.

Charlie had been quiet for a while, and I gathered that he was going through the same thoughts as mine. He sat up in his seat and lit a smoke. "Are we getting close?"

"Yeah, Charlie…real close. I want you to clean up the cockpit area and grab the seat cushions and our coats from the back."

He gave me a determined look of "Okay Skipper," but did not ask for an explanation. He knew it was to prepare for a possible crash landing into the woods of New Hampshire.

As we proceeded on our easterly heading the clouds began to take on an iridescent glow from below, and my eyes search for a bright glow indicating city lights. Charlie was getting excited over the potential good news and repeatedly talked on about how this was a good sign followed by "It's good…right, Andy?"

I kept my final descent plans into the clouds to myself until the very end as I did not want to dampen his spirits.

"Yeah, Charlie, looking good" was my positive response reply to his quizzical facial expressions. "Looking good."

At this time the sky brightened more from the glow below, and I spotted the C-130 circling left over the bright area. I pointed it out to Charlie. "Look twelve 'o clock…straight ahead…See the cargo plane?"

CHAPTER 26

FLIGHT 996 TO LONDON

I paused in the telling of the drama in the sky and suffered verbal abuse by my three captive audience members.

In unison, all three looked at me and shouted, "What happened next?"

I complained that I needed to use the "Blue Room" before I wet my pants from all the coffee I had been drinking that night. They complained about my timing, but of course my timing was perfect as I hope to have them on the edge of their seats a little longer than they wanted while they wait for my exciting finish of the story.

I went back and entered the forward lavatory right behind the cockpit door. I hated using these airborne toilets with their blue-colored chemical liquid instead of water for flushing the toilet. No matter how they drained the guck and serviced these facilities, they always stunk enough to make me almost gag. I was washing my hands when my reflection in the mirror actually stunned me.

Who is that? I thought. *That ain't me!*

Yeah…who was that looking back at me from the mirror? He looked old and tired, that surely was not Captain Andy Angelo. No way, I was a young captain enjoying my left seat position with all the benefits and challenges that came with that coveted position of four gold stripes on my arm sleeves.

Reality set in, and I reluctantly accepted my own image as it reflected back to me in the mirror. I washed my face and combed my thinning hair before I went back into the cabin. I grabbed another cup of coffee from Mary, but instead of going back into the cabin, I decided to walk through the cabin and visit the coach section flight attendants. I liked mingling with my crewmembers and for the most part they were always receptive with my visits. Invariably, a passenger would try to get my attention to ask me any question that would impress me with his knowledge of aviation.

I was always happy to oblige them as I consider it part of my duties to be a PR man for United Airlines. This night I was grabbed by the hand in business class by a very young English girl traveling with her mother. The mother was about to admonish her daughter, but I knelt beside the girl of about four or five to listen to what she wanted to ask or tell me.

"Are you the captain?" She had a very cute voice with a very upper class English accent. I smiled at her and gave her my standard wise guy answer.

"That's what they tell me." I could see that my answer confused her, so I gave her an answer that I should have given her in the first place.

"Yes, I am, and what is your name, pretty girl?"

She beamed at me calling her pretty girl; all females love compliments either young or old…makes no difference. She touched the stripes on my arm sleeve and asked me if they were real gold. The mother apologized for her daughter's question, but I decided to have a little fun and flirt with her mother who looked at least twenty years my junior.

"That's okay…Yes, they are real gold threads…You're very pretty like your beautiful mother. How old are you?"

What happened next completely caught me off guard. The mother spoke up telling me she was forty-two and the little girl just look incredulously at her mother.

"Mommy, the captain asked me, not you."

I started to laugh and her mother's face turned beet red while her daughter just glared at her.

I saved the situation and her mother's embarrassment over telling me her age.

"That's okay…Now tell me your age and your name," I whispered. "Tell me your mommy's name also."

She smiled at me and again gave her mother a disapproving look before answering me.

"My name is Cindy, I'm four years old." She looked up at her mother. "My mommy's name is Betty. What's your name?"

Betty's face turned more beet red than the first time, but she held her composure and began to again apologize for he daughter's questions. I waved it off and spoke to the daughter.

"You have a pretty name to match your pretty face like your mother. My name is Andrew."

"You're Captain Andrew?"

"No, I'm Captain Angelo, but you can call me Captain Andy." At this time, Mary answered the intercom phone and began to laugh. I heard her say, "You want me to say it like that?"

She laughed harder, hung up the phone, and walked toward me.

"Captain, I have a message from the cockpit."

I excused myself from my two new female friends and walked back toward the cockpit door while asking Mary what they wanted in the cockpit.

She laughed. "They said for you to get your ass back in your seat and finish the story. Are you telling more adventure stories of Captain Smiley's life?"

I knocked on the cockpit door while telling Mary, "Kelly will tell you the story when she returns to the cabin."

She barked, "Yeah, and when will that be?"

I teased back as the door opened, "Now…now…don't be jealous!"

I reentered the cockpit, sat in my seat, and asked, "Now where was I?"

They all screamed at me.

"You just saw the C-130 aircraft."

I teased, "Oh yeah…now I remember." I was really enjoying the moment as their faces reflected intense interest in my continuing the story.

"Yeah…I asked Charlie if he saw the C-130."

CHAPTER 27

ZERO TIME PLUS THREE HOURS

N6408Y

"Charlie, look…. twelve o' clock…straight ahead…the C-130. Do you see it?"

Charlie looked at the C-130, but saw that I was not heading toward it or the glow of the city lights. We didn't know if the large aircraft saw us, but as I explained the situation to Charlie, he realized it was a moot point.

"Charlie, we can't let down directly over the glow…that's Manchester…too many large buildings. I don't know our fuel remaining."

I explained my fear of losing control in the descent and crashing into buildings and killing people on the ground. Charlie let out a long sigh and asked me what my plan entailed to get us through the clouds.

I was very familiar with the Nashua Airport area as it was the airport I used to first solo student pilots, and I also used it to train advanced multiengine pilots on operating the aircrafts with loss of one engine. The runway was a good 5,000 feet long and aligned north and south as was common in New England due to its large percentage of northeast winds. The main advantage was that the north end of the airport was almost devoid of obstructions and the clearing to the approach to runway 14 would allow me to get down to the "deck" below most clouds. I purposely chose to descend north of the airport to take advantage of the terrain, and I wasn't concerned with the wind direction because of the Aztec having a slow approach speed and of the length of the runway.

After informing Charlie, he understood the situation. "Okay, Skipper, you're the boss. How are we going to descend?"

My plan was to slow the aircraft to just above an aerodynamic stall by getting it to a stall buffet and then correcting it to just above the stall speed. The airspeed indicator was unreliable, and this was a good way to reduce our forward speed, and it could be used for the approach speed. The only danger was that this procedure required both engines to be running properly. If we loss either engine due to fuel starvation, I would have to increase the speed in order to gain control of the Aztec.

The flaps and landing gear on the Aztec were driven by engine-geared mechanical hydraulic pumps, and they should operate normally on selection by me. I was to set the flaps to about ten degrees as this would create more lift than drag and allow me to fly the bird at a slightly lower speed with a less pitch up nose attitude for better forward visibility.

We would descend no higher than 500 feet per minute to 1,500 feet altimeter reading and then I would reduce the vertical rate to 100 to 200 feet per minute while maintaining the slowest forward speed as possible. This would give us a higher chance of survival if we hit any trees or the ground before we got visual ground contact. I would start off with a very shallow 10 degrees of bank either left or right while descending, but at 1,500 feet indicated I would align the aircraft on a southerly heading of 180 degrees. The logic was that we would still be north of the airport while descending and the southerly heading would be taking us to the airport and it should have us lined up for a straight in approach to runway 14.

I instructed Charlie that he was to hold the cloth-covered lens flashlight on the instrument panel and when I told him to kill the light to not hesitate.

He shrugged his shoulders. "Anything else you want me to do?"

"Yeah…keep positive thoughts, stay alert, stay focused."

Charlie smiled at me and answered, "Piece of cake."

I now gave Charlie a decision he would have to make before the descent.

I told him that his chances of surviving a crash would be greatly enhanced if he stacked our clothing and some of the rear seat cushions between him and the instrument panel. This would greatly decrease his impact from the crash.

He looked at me. "How the hell am I going to look for the airport and ground if I do that?"

I just looked at him. "You're not, but it could save your ass."

Charlie got angry at me and yelled at me, "Fuck that shit. We're a team, right? I'm looking out with you!"

I was glad he decided on that action as it would help to have his eyeballs looking out while I had to switch from inside and outside the aircraft in order to keep it in the flight envelop I set up for the descent.

I took a couple of deep breaths. "Okay, let's do it!"

We entered the clouds at about 9,500 feet.

CHAPTER 28

ZERO TIME PLUS THREE HOURS AND TEN MINUTES

ARTCC, C-130, ASR CHOPPER, AZTEC

The transmission had been made to Boston ATC control that the Aztec had been seen descending through the cloud due west of the position of the ASR chopper and the Pacer 02 aircraft orbiting the KMHT airport area.

Sal's screaming question of, "Does he see you? Does he see you?" was answered by the Pacer 02 Colonel Winters. "We can't tell. He gave no signal to us. We're heading toward his descent position now."

The ASR chopper began to scream over the radio, "God damn it where did he descend? What position?" At the same time, the chopper pilot slammed the twin turbine engines to maximum power to fly to the area where the Pacer 02 aircraft reported the Aztec was descending.

The Boston controllers were all up on their feet while Sal paced the floor swearing. "God Damn it, we don't know if he's out of fuel or he is descending on purpose. Somebody give me his estimated fuel left."

John left the now blank radar scope, which no longer had the Aztec showing in a return and walked to Sal. "Sal, he should have been tanks dry ten minutes ago according to his stated FOB to TEB."

Sal looked at John. "Do you think he ran out of fuel?"

"I don't know. Let's ask the Pacer 02 aircraft."

Sal grabbed the mic and asked Winters if he could tell if the Aztec was under power when he descended; he gave an encouraging answer. He reflected that the pilot seemed too much in control to let his fuel run dry without attempting to make a control descent and that he thought that they descended west of Manchester to avoid the city and crashing into buildings.

Sal acknowledged Winters's opinion and pondered the facts of the Pacer's assertion of N6408Y actions. If true the pilot has "brass balls" and a very cool demeanor to carry out this decision, which Sal thought decreased their chance of survival. John verified to Sal the loss of the radar target, which indicated that the Aztec was now below target acquisition height.

Meanwhile, the chopper had arrived over the descent position of the Aztec with Williams briefing his crew.

"We're making a zero visibility descent over the twin's last position down to 150 feet AGL on the radar altimeter. Stay alert...I want all eyeballs outside!"

The Aztec was descending in its shallow left-hand turn with a sink rate of about 500 feet per minute. The descent started out smooth, but as we descended through 5,000 feet, we started to get turbulence causing Charlie to cinch his seat belt tighter.

I was concentrating on my pitch and bank angle and nervously checking my altitude when it occurred to me that the altimeter reading would be off due to us not having an accurate pressure setting.

Without any warning, my mind wandered to the thought of being dead and in eternal darkness. The fear was physically overwhelming as it began in my left foot as a feeling of an electric shock and traveled up my body, causing me to gasp as it passed through my chest and out the top of my head. It left me dazed and a feeling of exhaustion came over me. As usual when I am confronted with danger or an uncertain precarious position, I become angry. This anger

caused me to burst out in a barrage of profanities. "Fuck this shit…
Ain't anybody dying tonight…No fucking way!"

Charlie quickly responded to my outburst, "Fucking, A!"

The ASR chopper started its descent with the commander briefing his cockpit crew while they were descending. "Watch our sink
rate…No more than 500 feet per minute…When the radar altimeter
comes alive at 2,500 AGL, let me know."

The chopper began to feel the lower level chop from the surface
winds blowing over the terrain and Williams is having difficulty controlling his sink rate.

He shouted, "Shit, this is bad. What's our AGL?"

His copilot answered, "We're at 1,500 feet AGL sinking minus
500."

Bill angrily responded, "Where the fuck was my 2,500 foot call?
Get with it before we bust our asses!"

The chopper crew is straining their eyes to see through the
clouds and fog. Their faces are pressed up against the bubble plexiglas
observers' windows.

The Boston control room has become quiet and a somber
mood has spread throughout the controllers. It has the atmosphere
of a funeral wake as the men begin to get a welling of moisture in
their eyes. A constant clearing of throats, a slight shallow cough,
a soft muttering of profanities, and a hiding of one's face to avoid
eye contact with another controller. They were hiding the emotions
screaming inside them from the frustration of being so close to a rescue and losing at the very end to the odds against them succeeding
in the rescue.

"Boston Center…Pacer 02…Say instructions." Sal sat unre-
sponsive to the transmission by Winters. He was numb to be so close
and to fail; it was too much for him to handle at that moment. He
slowly lifted from his chair and walked silently to an exit leading to
a stair well. He grabbed the knob and looked back at his men in the
control room before turning the knob and exiting the room.

John took control of the room and talked to the rescue team.

The Aztec was encountering some wind buffeting, causing me
to begin to sweat with my efforts of remaining in control of the entire

situation. My sense had been shocked by my fear, but the fear only heightened my senses and sped up my reaction time. I was ready to react to anything and calmness came over me.

No more thinking, only a pure physical reaction would save us tonight…I was pumped and ready!

The descent morphed into slow motion and the outside world got quiet as the only sound that I was hearing was our breathing. As we passed 1,500 feet, I instructed Charlie to shut off the light, and I leveled the wings on a heading of due south, 180 degrees on the directional compass.

I slowed our descent to 200 feet per minute and ever so slowly we inched our way toward the ground. As the altimeter read 200 feet, a sudden violent slamming of the under belly of the aircraft was followed by a loud scrapping with a *WHACK, WHACK* as it became obvious that the Aztec was skimming the top of the trees north of the airport. I immediately pulled the nose up, added power, and we began a life-and-death dance with the treetops as ground contact began to come in view.

As we climbed, it suddenly appeared that we were in a very narrow band of clear sky with visibility good enough to see forward for about two miles. It was if we were flying in a tube of clear air and the tunnel vision view was quite evident as I tried to stay out of the trees, but remain contact with the ground.

After about one minute of dancing with the treetops, the ground sloped down and the most beautiful sight in the world was seen dead ahead.

"Charlie, look! Look it's a goddamn runway!" The runway appeared with all its light to full intensity to say, "Get that aircraft over here now!"

Charlie began to holler in his excitement, and I admonished him. "Not now. The flight's not over until we park the plane."

There was no way I was going to screw this up now. I decided to keep the flap setting the same as I didn't know if we had sustained any damage to the flaps or under wing area. I recognized the Nashua airport and the runway. We had nailed our position exactly where we needed to be, just north of the Nashua airport.

I had no airspeed indicator, but the speed felt correct as we got lower and lower to touching down onto the south heading runway at Nashua Airport. The altimeter read zero while still about 100 feet in the air and coupled with the airport's altitude our altimeter reading was off about 300 feet due to not having the proper pressure setting.

I lowered the landing gear and was shocked to see the three small green lights of it being down and locked illuminate. Evidently the battery had recovered some of its power during the shutdown of all the electrical systems, but it quickly went out.

As I looked at the runway coming over the threshold, the runway appeared to be wet and as soon as we touched down it became apparent why it was so shiny; it was a sheet of black ice. As I applied the rudder pedal brakes, I had no feeling in my frozen feet, which caused me to unevenly apply the almost useless brakes due to the ice. I was using differential power to keep the Aztec going down the centerline, and as we got farther down the runway, the wheels began to grab a piece of the asphalt as we chirped and slid down the runway.

As we approached the end of the runway, I shut both engines down through their fuel control levers and kicked hard right rudder while trying to lock the right wheel brake. It worked as we made a hard right turn into the ramp area making a 180 degree turn in the parking area.

We came to a sudden stop!

Silence! Charlie looked at me and screamed, "You gotta be fucking shitting me!" He uttered every obscenity, and we both began to celebrate on beating tremendous odds and surviving the horrific flight.

We were alive…the feeling was overwhelming…*We were alive!*

The chopper was still making its descent into the area the Aztec was last seen north of Nashua Airport.

Bill asked his copilot to read off the radar altimeter altitude and to call out an abort at 150 feet AGL.

Copilot read, "Skipper…300, 250, 225, 200, 175…150…pull up pull up!"

Williams threw the twin turbine engines to max power. They quickly spool up and let out a screaming sound as Williams adjusted the collective pitch and controls of the big ASR chopper to stop its descent and to climb to a safe altitude.

The chopper climbed back up to 9,000 feet and headed toward the Pacer 02 aircraft.

Williams reports to the Boston ARTCC.

"Boston, we went down to 150 feet AGL…We never saw the ground. My guess is they crashed into the woods north of the airport. We can stay on station for about an hour to help with the recovery ground crews."

"Boston…Pacer 02…We need to head into Bedford…We're low on fuel…Sorry we didn't get a good ending."

John answered the flight rescue team, "Thanks, guys…super effort."

The chopper responded, "Yeah…super effort…negative results…GODDAMN IT!"

John released the ASR and Pacer 02 from the rescue effort, and he had the appropriate FAA facilities notified of the tragic conclusion of the rescue attempt of N6408Y. He notified the New Hampshire State Police of the crash site and other ground recovery units located near Nashua.

Sal had stepped to the rear wall of the stairwell and leaned against the wall slowly lowering his massive frame into a seating knelling position. He rubs a hand continuously over his burr cut head while holding his face in the other hand. He is completely spent, physically and mentally, while his mind screams inside his head.

"Why…why…It isn't fair!" It was too much of a burden to handle at that moment as his mind also wandered back to that night in Germany. Sal was reduced to a sobbing hulk of a defeated man as he sat alone in the cold on the stair well floor.

Charlie and I sat quietly in the cockpit of the Aztec after our jubilant profane-laden screams finally ended. I sat reflecting on the many seemingly unconnected incidents to the flight that had contributed to our safe landing. I checked my watch; we had been in the air almost three hours and thirty minutes well beyond my estimate of dry tanks at three hours. The runaway prop, which had acted up early in the flight, had me reducing the power to just about idle on the right engine. This was not calculated in my three-hour estimate of FOB in my mayday message to TEB Airport.

The incident at Keene Airport on spotting the Northeast Airliner and the wild ride that ensued contributed greatly to our survival this night. The prop had freed itself from the full lock forward position and gave us back full power in both engines. The airliner sighting had showed me our actual position and not our calculated position. The wind being stronger from the east and the constant heading deviations to avoid clouds and the icing conditions had us much farther to the west over dangerous hills.

The spotting of the city lights just prior to the Aztec stalling at 23,000 feet. The fact that we actually reached that height to clear the tops of the clouds was aided by the strong updrafts from the building lower cumulus cloud.

The logic that the rescue aircraft had used to seek our aircraft at different altitudes, which resulted in my confirming of heading east toward Manchester Airport as we followed the Pacer 02 aircraft… contributed to our survival.

My familiarity with the Nashua Airport and the surrounding area from my flight instructing at Executive Flyers Aviation at the Bedford Airport was a huge factor in my decision making on our final almost suicidal descent.

All these factors contributed along with Charlie Califf being my passenger to our surviving and beating the odds against us.

The fact that I was young and in excellent physical condition to be able to handle the physical and mental load imposed on me during the night contributed to our survival. The unexplained hearing of my father's voice screaming in my ears, "Butch…Butch… Wake up!" contributed to our survival.

The total rescue efforts by all that night, FAA, Air Force, Coast Guard, they all contributed to a happy ending, but Charlie and I both knew, *we pulled our survival out of our asses!*

We were goddamn lucky to be alive!

CHAPTER 29

POST FLIGHT

Nashua Airport, FAA Boston Center

We exited the Aztec with a sense of unbelievable joy of being alive. I walked to the wing tank filler caps to get a visual on the fuel left in the tanks. I took my pen flashlight and shined into the filler hole on the left wing; I could see no reflection indicating any fuel in the tank. I went to the right tank and repeated my efforts, which resulted in seeing a few wet spots on the bottom of the tank. We were basically dry tanks, zero remaining fuel to burn.

Charlie grasped my faces with both hands and began to attack my cheeks with a barrage of kisses from the joy of just realizing how truly close we were to auger dead stick with no power into the treetops.

I begged Charlie to stop, "Christ, Charlie, we'll need a motel room if you keep this up."

My eyes were surveying the area to make sure we had no witness to this event thus getting the wrong impression of why two men were kissing on the parking ramp apron.

Charlie laughed at my comment, which of course led me to join in his laughter.

We began walking toward the small airport terminal when I got shooting pains in both of my feet. My feet were beginning to thaw out, which caused this shooting pain. I started to stumble, and

Charlie put his arm under me to help me as I hobbled toward the terminal.

"Jesus, kid, you okay?"

I explained to him about my feet, and he gave me a very sympathetic look.

"Why didn't you tell me?" I just shrugged my shoulders while noticing that I was now "The Kid" again in Charlie's mind.

We entered the terminal where two middle-aged men were sitting around an aviation radio frequency receiver drinking coffee. They were intensely listening to "chatter" from an aircraft over head the airport when one of the men looked up and gave us a confused stare.

"Hey…where did you guys come from?"

I started to laugh, but answered, "We just landed."

He bellowed back, "What? You just landed!"

Charlie began to laugh as I spit out, "Yeah…we just landed… Where's your men's room?"

He would not let it go. "The airport is closed due to freezing rain…an aircraft is lost in the area tying up the entire northeast flight corridor and…you just landed?"

I again replied with an edge to my voice, "Yeah, we just landed. Where's your head located?"

He looked back at me more confused as I used the navy term *head* meaning men's room.

I got his not knowing the term. "Look, man, tell me where I can take a piss and put some warm water on my frozen feet!"

Charlie added his two cents worth into the conversation, "Just tell us where the john is located!"

He pointed to the right rear side of the terminal, and we proceeded to the facilities; I turned my head around and shouted back at the men, "That wouldn't be an Aztec N6408Y that's causing all the commotion, is it?"

They shouted back, "Yeah, they've been trying to get him on the ground for hours. You know them?"

"You're talking to them." My reply resulted in a stare of disbelief as Charlie and I entered the men's room. I didn't know what to do first, urinate or soak my feet, but thanks to my mother's toilet training me by holding my hands under the faucet to get me to pee before going to bed I opted to relieve myself before soaking my feet. It would most definitely ruin my macho image if I wet my pants and told my heroic flight with a wet crotch.

I took off my shoes and socks and sat up on a radiator to soak my feet in the warm water of the sink. Man, it hurt a lot, and Charlie could see the pain on my face as he kept asking how he could help me. In about five minutes, my feet began to turn pink from a whitish dull color indicating that the blood was now flowing freely in my feet. I wiped my feet with paper towels, and Charlie and I left the men's room with me holding my socks and shoes in my hands.

When we returned to the main terminal area, we had an increase in our audience of five more men dressed in various colored overalls. A few aircraft mechanics and the airport cleaning staff were staring at us as we made our way to the well-worn sofa in the room. A few more men came into the terminal as one of the men had made a call to some local pilot friends.

They all started to ask question at the same time—who, what, how, when, and so on and so on.

I held up my hand to stop all the questions and asked if they had a phone we could use to notify the FAA of our landing in Nashua as they were probably sending out ground vehicles to locate the crash site.

This got their immediate attention, and they led me barefoot with Charlie in tow to a phone on the front desk. It was a direct line to the FAA Boston ARTCC located in Nashua, New Hampshire.

I picked up the phone, and Charlie pulled my hand so as he could also listen in on the conversation.

It rang and after a few rings someone answered the phone. "Boston Center…John O'Brien here." His voice sounded stressed, and without thinking, I asked him what's the matter.

He replied in a totally defeated tone. "We've been attempting for hours to rescue a light twin, but it appears he crashed just north of the Nashua Airport. Who am I talking to, and how can I help you?"

I answered back, "Well, who am I talking to?"

He answered a little annoyed, "You're talking to the acting shift supervisor. Now who are you, and how can I help you?"

Charlie was laughing, but urged me to end the poor man's suffering.

"Well, Mister Acting Supervisor, you're talking to Andy Angelo, the pilot of Aztec N6408Y...that's who!"

It took a long second before he shouted into the mouthpiece. "What?"

"I'm the pilot of N6408Y...You know, the one you assumed crashed into the woods. Well you can call off the ground search for the wreckage and bodies. We landed at the Nashua Airport about fifteen minutes ago."

After a long pause with no response...I said, "Hey, Mister FAA man, you copy?"

"Yeah, I copy. Don't go anywhere. I'm sending a car to get you at the airport. I need you to talk to somebody. Don't hang up."

Charlie looked amused at John's tone and request, but did not say anything as I answered John, "Okay, I'll wait for the car, and I'll hang on the phone. We can't go anywhere we have no car."

He excitedly answered, "Yeah okay...Stay on the line."

I cupped the mouthpiece and talked to Charlie. "Did you get all that?"

"Yeah...they're sending a car and for Christ's sake don't hang up!"

I looked around the room as the men were just itching to start their barrage of questions at Charlie and me.

John placed my call on hold and warned the other controllers not to touch the phone as he went looking for Sal. He first went to the stairwell, but Sal was not in the area. John then proceeded to Sal's office where he found him sitting in his swivel chair rocking back and forth just staring at the wall. Sal did not notice John entering the room, and when John cleared his throat, it startled Sal.

"Christ, John, stop sneaking up on me!"

John ignored him. "Sal, you need to talk to someone on the phone from the Nashua Airport."

Sal stood up and looked at John. "Who wants to talk to me?"

"I don't know...They didn't say."

"What do you mean they didn't say? Christ, John, I'm not in the fucking mood to talk to anyone."

"Sal...He said he can only talk to you."

"What...He said 'I have to talk to Sal Rizzo'?"

"No...you know, Sal, he asked for the supervisor."

Sal resigned to taking the phone call, and he began to walk toward the phone with John. The other controllers were quiet as they suspected by John's demeanor after the phone call that some news about the accident was going to come over the phone line.

John pointed to the phone on hold and slipped away to the phone button that would put the telephone on the room's loud speakers.

Sal picked up the phone. "Sal Rizzo, here."

Charlie and I both heard the exhausted voice of Sal Rizzo, and I stated, "Okay...You're Sal Rizzo...Who are you?"

He quickly answered, "I'm not in the mood to play games. I'm Sal Rizzo, senior FAA Boston supervisor. Who the hell are you?"

At this time John connected the phone to the control room speakers.

I answered, "Mister Rizzo, you're talking to Andy Angelo, the pilot of Aztec N6408Y...that's who!"

I heard the echo from the loud speakers and a deafening roar of people yelling, whistling, and hand clapping.

I laughed and told Charlie they must be glad we're alive. He answered me, "Not as glad as us."

Rizzo held the phone high above his head and shouted, "They made it! Jesus Christ they're alive...They made it!"

John went over to Sal and put his arms around the exhausted man who had tears coming down his face. The men all got emotional and the cheers turned to a quiet thanks to all their fellow controllers.

John told Sal that he was going to send a car to the Nashua Airport to picked us up and bring them to the center.

Sal nodded his head and quietly spoke to me, "We're so glad you made it...Congratulations."

I didn't know what to say but…"Thanks…same to you."

Sal handed the phone back to John. "I need to sit. Let me know when they get here."

John took the phone and patted Sal on his shoulder. "We did good tonight, Sal."

Sal answered, "No, they did good. They saved themselves."

He left for his office as John told me that they would be at the airport in less than thirty minutes.

He just said goodbye and hung up.

Charlie and I just realized at that second that we were not the only ones caught up in our drama, but all that tried to rescue us were feeling the same tension and the final release of a happy ending.

While waiting for the FAA car, we began to talk to the men in the terminal about the flight. The response from the pilots in the group was exactly what I knew it was going to be in response to some of the details of the flight—second-guessing and Monday morning quarter backing with a lot of disbelief of the details. It was quite amusing for me to watch and listen to these pilots discuss what they would have done in our situation as all pilots want to measure their imagined superior piloting skills against other pilots. They cannot resist the urge to "puff out their chests" and proudly proclaim, "This is what you should have done."

Charlie was not amused and angrily stated, "You have no idea what happened to us. That kid is the best goddamn pilot you will ever meet in your life!" I quieted Charlie by putting my finger to my lips and gave him a slight shush sound, but I smiled in appreciation of his sincere comments.

I heard a squealing of car brakes and looked out the window to see car lights pulling into the parking lot. They were going so fast I thought they were going to crash into the terminal building. Three men leaped from the auto and dashed into the terminal and simultaneously shouted, "We're looking for Andy Angelo!"

The men in the room all pivoted and looked at me, which resulted in the FAA personnel descending on me with their hands extended and huge smiles on their faces.

One quipped, "He's just a kid."

Good old Charlie came to my defense one more time, "No, he's young...but a man...not a kid."

The controller's face blushed, and I laughed to myself as Charlie was always calling me a kid; I guess when you save a man's life you go up a notch in manhood.

CHAPTER 30

THANK YOU AND CELEBRATION

They quickly ushered us into their vehicle as the men in the terminal congratulated us; I guessed for being alive. A constant stream of questions began as we began the short drive to the FAA center; what, why, how until I just asked them to let Charlie and me try to relax on the ride to the center. They apologized and complied with my request with a subdued, "Sorry, we're just excited that you guys are alive."

We arrived at the Control Center and entered the bomb-proof building housing an array of analog computers, radar screens, communication system, and the many types of personnel required to operate and maintain the various pieces of equipment.

As we walked into the main control room, I was surprised how quiet the room was with only the occasional staccato of a teletype machine punching out some information on its roll of paper. No one was talking, not between themselves or for that matter into their transmitter microphones to controlled aircraft.

Without any warning, one of the FAA controllers from the automobile trip shouted, "These are the guys from N6408Y!" This caused an explosive sound of hand clapping, whistles, and loud shouts of joy on our safe arrival on the ground. We shook many hands and received a hundred slaps on our backs with the obligatory…"Well done. Congratulations!"

I was amused when I heard whispered several times, "Which one is the pilot?"

I kidded one by pointing at Charlie and saying, "The pilot's name is Angelo. Does he look like an Angelo to you?" It brought quite a bit of laughter, but then the room quieted and I saw this hulking figure slowly make his way toward us. With that face and exhausted look, I knew it had to be Sal Rizzo. He was walking with John, and as they approached us, they both began to smile at me. As if it was rehearsed that the smiles were a cue for another round of applause; it began as a quiet slow clapping of the hands with a steady increase in tempo and volume the closer Sal got to me. When he reached for my hand and put his massive hand on my shoulder, the room once again erupted into a cacophony of voices and whistling.

After fielding a thousand questions, Sal pulled me and Charlie aside. "I have two pilots who wish to congratulate you on your professionalism."

We walked to a table with variety of phones, and Sal picked one of them up and handed to me. I said hello and asked who was on the phone.

He quickly responded, "Colonel Winters, commander of Pacer 02 C-130...Are you the pilot in command of 6408Y?" I smiled at the pilot in command reference to me and said, "Yes."

"That was one sweet job you did of not buying the farm tonight, young man." An old expression long used by the aviation community..."Buying the farm," meaning to crash and die, was probably held over from the early "barnstorming days" of early aviation.

"Thanks, Colonel...did my best to stay alive."

He laughed at my response, and after several personal questions by the colonel of my age and flight experience, he made reference to my naval aviation experience.

"Always glad to help out you navy types to stay above ground and not buried in it." This was followed by a "well done" comment.

"Yes, sir...same to you. Thanks."

This same conversation was duplicated with Commander Williams, the commander of the Cape Cod ASR Helicopter Squadron, but with the kidding being about the air force pilots and not about naval aviators. The Coast Guard aviators received their flight training with the naval aviators, and we considered them to be one of us.

The competition between pilots is always present especially between the different military branches.

After we verified the transcripts of the flight and just about wore out my fingers from shaking hands, the off-going duty FAA controllers declared that they had to get Charlie and me totally drunk. We took one last Polaroid picture and a large number of us headed to the bar at the nearby Holiday Inn. I was more concerned about getting some food in me as Charlie and I had not eaten since early morning and my stomach was beginning to growl.

We took over the entire bar area at the Holiday Inn with ordering food and drinks for quite a few of the controllers whose numbers increased as they got off duty at the center. After a few drinks and a lot of food, I realized that we had no transportation to our cars parked at the Bedford Airport.

Charlie calmed my fear of being up all night with the controllers when he told me a company car was on its way to pick us up and take us to Bedford. I excused myself from the room and proceeded to a pay phone to call my wife.

I dialed long distance collect hoping that Janet was still awake as it was now after 11:00 PM, and she had difficulty staying awake after 10:00 PM.

The phone rang a few times, and she picked up the receiver.

A sleepy voice spoke, "Hello."

"Long distance collect call from a Mr. Angelo…Will you accept the charges?"

"Yes."

"Go ahead, sir."

"Hey, babe, were you sleeping?"

"What time is it?"

"Late a little after 11:00."

"Where are you?"

"I'm in Nashua, New Hampshire."

"Where?"

I started to laugh at this clipped way of conversing with Janet and just told her we had a few problems with the aircraft and that we had to land in New Hampshire and not Bedford. I told her not to worry; I would be home late and to not wait up for me.

She laughed. "I stopped worrying and staying awake for you years ago."

I teased her a little then asked her, "You still love me?"

"Yeah, but don't wake me when you get home." Again, the code for no sex tonight.

I laughed at her coded message, and we said our goodbyes.

Our ride arrived at around midnight, and after we begged off any more drinks, we said goodbye to a mostly wasted crew of FAA controllers. It was obvious to me that this was a common watering hole for the FAA personnel at the center and that they spent many a night here unwinding before heading home.

The ride to Bedford was about forty-five minutes, and with the alcohol and fatigue setting in, I quickly began to doze off, but not before my mind made a quick recap of the entire night's events.

I had met the ultimate tests of challenges that would have killed a less capable or level-headed pilot. I was proud of my actions and personal behavior during this dangerous flight.

I was also proud of Charlie and his mostly cool manner he displayed as we confronted each circumstance that had the potential of being fatal.

We were lucky that night, but we were also very good.

I mentally gave us a "well done" and slipped into sleep.

I was woken by the slamming of the car door and saw that we were in the Bedford Airport parking lot. I got out of the car followed by Charlie, and we walked together to our cars without saying a word. Charlie walked me to my car, put his arm around my shoulder, and said, "You did good tonight, kid."

"No, Charlie...We both did good tonight." He smiled at me and without saying another word headed to his car. We departed the airport for our drives to our homes, each with our own thoughts of the night's flight.

The ride to my home had me at the door at about 3:00 am; I quietly slipped the key into the door lock and squeezed the door opened. I went to my children's shared bedroom and watched them sleeping for a few minutes before I adjusted their bed covers. I did not become emotional, but I was damn happy to see them.

I entered my bedroom and heard the soft breathing of my wife, and as quietly as possible, I began to undress. Obviously, not quiet enough…

Janet quizzed me, "Is that you?"

"No…it's the guy next door."

She teased, "Hurry before my husband gets home."

I turned to the bed to see Janet leaning on her elbow looking at me with a gleam in her eyes.

I crawled under the covers and said, "You gotta be kidding me."

She wrapped her body around me and teased, "You're getting old."

I suddenly became totally exhausted, and as I began to drift asleep, I said, "You almost became a widow tonight."

"Don't worry, I'll kill you for some reason before you make me a widow."

I smiled while our bodies came together like two spoons in a draw, and I slowly slipped into the comfort of a peaceful sleep.

CHAPTER 31

UNITED FLIGHT 996

The storytelling had ended, and I now was waiting for the word I knew was going to be uttered from one of my audience's mouth. I said nothing, and they just looked at me while absorbing the details of the flight.

I pushed my seat back and put my feet up under the instrument panel and remained quiet.

It's coming...wait for it...wait for it...

The word I knew was going to be first spoken stammered out from the least expected mouth; Kelly's.

Kelly stammered, "But..."

I jumped in before she could say another word.

"But what?"

"But..."

I started to laugh as Kelly looked at Joe and Frank for help, but they did not offer any words to her "But."

I finished her question for her, "But, Captain, why didn't you fly to the coast over the water and descend?"

The look on Kelly's face was priceless; she must have thought I was a mind reader, but in reality, every time I told this story to pilots and non-pilots invariable this question got asked...always. The expression on Frank and Joe's faces asked me the same question while I told Kelly that her question was asked by all who heard the story of the flight. I imagined that all the listeners were subconsciously putting themselves in my position and trying to decide their best course of action.

I left the question hang in the air until Frank said, "Yeah, Captain, seems like a good idea to me."

I now had to educate my three listeners to the dangers of flying over water at night under a cloud deck. I had over 3,500 flight hours as a flight member on Navy P3 Orion aircraft over the Pacific Ocean flying as low as 100 feet in total pitch darkness as we conducted our patrols searching for Russian submarines or other duties while in Vietnam. I explained that night flying over the water requires full aircraft instruments and the most essential piece of equipment was a "radar altimeter", which sends a radar signal to the surface and by measuring its return calculates the actual height above the surface, AGL. We, of course, had this equipment on our Boeing, and it was an integral piece of equipment used not only for a visual and aural indication or warnings but tied into many flight systems. It was automatically activated at 2,500 feet above the surface.

The barometric altimeter depends on local barometric pressure settings in inches or other references, and it shows you an altitude reading above the reference set in the altimeter.

The Aztec had neither an accurate altimeter setting nor a radar altimeter, making it far too dangerous a course of action to descend hoping to see something on the surface for a height reference. There would be a good chance of simply flying the Aztec into the water and even if we survived the crash the cold November water temperatures would have had us drowning in a very short time.

I told them the story of how, while on patrol over the waters of Vietnam, we had been dropping flares in the water looking for some debris from one of our aircraft that reportedly had crashed into the sea, which almost led to our own crashing into the water.

I had walked into the cockpit scanning the flight instruments while the PIC was looking out the cockpit window pivoting on what he thought was a flare, but in reality was a far off star, which appeared to be on the surface. We were 500 feet off the ocean's surface in a descending 45 degree angle of bank headed for a crash into the sea. I screamed out a warning, and he corrected the aircraft to straight and level flight. If I had not, by good fortune entered the cockpit at that precise time to scream the warning, we would have flown into the water. The copilot had dozed off for a few seconds and jumped as I screamed out the warning. The PIC climbed the P3 up to 1,500 feet and just said, "Thanks."

It is very easy to get disoriented over the water at night especially under a cloud deck. The idea of letting down off the coast hoping to pick up city lights for a visual reference was ruled out by me one minute into the flight.

This explanation quieted my audience, but I was waiting for the next salvo of questions when Mary knocked on the cockpit door to be let into the cockpit. Kelly opened the door, and as Mary entered, she excitedly exclaimed, "Mary, you should have heard the story the captain just told us!"

Mary's response was sharp, "Well, some of us actually have to work this flight tonight and can't spare the time to be entertained by Captain Angelo."

I knew she was angry with me for her perception of usurping her cabin authority by allowing Kelly to stay "up front," but before she went on a rampage, I injected, "Kelly said she is feeling much better now. She's able to resume her cabin duties." I hoped that Kelly took the clue, and I was relieved when she chimed in, "Right, Captain. I'm feeling a lot better." She got up to leave the cockpit and turned around while smiling at me… "Captain, your story ending gives you away as a romantic."

The other two winced when she said it, but I gave my standard reply when accused of being a romantic, "No sense being Italian if you aren't."

Kelly exited and Mary quickly began to berate me more than the situation with Kelly warranted.

"Well, Captain, I hope you had fun entertaining Kelly with your 'oh gosh there I was tales,' and now I have to discipline her to get her back to work."

There is an unspoken understood rule between the "front office" and rear cabin on separation of authority, but Mary was about to discover that Captain Smiley took his ultimate authority very seriously.

I forcefully told Mary that she will do no such thing and to just let Kelly do her cabin duties. I told her that she was negligent by even allowing an obviously sick Kelly to be on board the flight in the first place. She should have been removed from our trip as we had more than the legal minimum FAs on board for the trip to London. Any bullshit of Kelly being in the cockpit requiring more work by the other FAs did not hold water.

It got very quiet while Joe and Frank began to do imaginary flight duties; I waited for a reply or a tirade of accusations of me exceeding my authority over her cabin crew, but nothing!

Not even acknowledgment of my anger, just a quiet stare from Mary and then it started, a quivering of her bottom lip, a swelling of dew in her eyes, and an expression in her face of a little girl about to burst out in full blown sobs and tears. She began to cry and sob loudly, causing her eye mascara to quickly run down her face, leaving streaks of black on her cheeks. I was shocked as I did not see this coming at all. Christ, this was getting out of hand, and I looked for Joe and Frank for help. They just looked bewildered and shrugged their shoulders and quickly went back to their imagined necessary duties of checking every overhead button and switch on the Boeing. I curse to myself. "You chicken shits…You'll pay for abandoning me in my hour of need!"

I got out of my seat, and Mary quickly came to me and cried, "I'm sorry, Andy."

Ah, she called me Andy, a good sign. "What's up, Mary?"

She begged off my question and just admitted to just not being "herself" the last few days.

She began to wipe her eyes. "Andy, I don't want to go into my personal problems."

That was fine by me; God knows what was really causing this crying out burst and cruising at 35,000 feet over the Atlantic with a plane full of paying passengers was not a great place to find out.

We hugged to indicate that we were both good with each other again, and she left the cockpit. I now turned my attention on my two first officers who had sunk a little lower in their seats in anticipation of a little ass kicking by the old guy in command.

I started, "Jesus, guys, a little freaking help would have been appreciated!"

Joe quickly responded, "Shit…No way I was getting involved in that mess." Frank just nodded his head in agreement.

I berated them more for not helping to diffuse the situation, and I warned them that their "left seat" future position would be hell if they had no insight how to deal with the FAs, male or female. I told them that being a captain is like having fifteen to twenty-two wives on board with each international flight. You're locked in a room with them with nowhere to hide.

The age mix of the FAs was from being just a kid like Kelly to FAs older than any of the pilots with a variety in between them representing a variety of backgrounds.

Half of a captain's duties were to keep the back end of the airplane happy and doing their duties. They could act up on occasion as spoiled kids or jealous wives and get into verbal cat fights with each other, not good for the passengers. On long international flights, you had to be aware of any problem with your cabin crew.

I looked at Joe and Frank and half serious, half kidding, "Chicken shits, both of you."

The incident put a slight dampening on an otherwise great evening flight with the reminiscing of my younger adventurous glory days. Whatever was bothering Mary would have to wait until I got off flight deck duty.

I told Frank to go into the cabin and to at least try to rest before he had to relieve Joe from his first officer's duty. Fatigue can be very insidious after flying a long flight and, depending on countless variables, affect a pilot's capacity to function at a required level for safety.

I prided myself on always maximizing my endurance capacity by following a regimented fitness program of exercising and running since I was in my early teens. I had inherited my father's vainness on his perceived superior physique and strength and even when he suffered from the effects of his Parkinson's Disease he tried to do his pushups and swim at the local YMCA. I laughed with my pop as he proudly read a *Boston Globe* sport's articled named, "Where Are They

Now" and his name appeared as "Hard as Nails Angelo" from his glory days as captain of his high school football team.

My father was one tough SOB, and he never once complained to me, any of my siblings, or my mother about this dreaded disease. He deserved a better ending to his life.

The remaining flight time fell into its normal desired routine and the hours passed quickly without any further incidents from the cabin or inflight abnormal situations. I went into the cabin during my rest period and sat in the seat reserved for flight crew rest, seat 2A. I placed my feet under a blanket, put my hat over my eyes, and much to my surprise, I fell easily to sleep. I guess all the talking of the past and the dream I had about my father on the deadheading from Boston stirred up the dream of the most exciting day of my young life.

CHAPTER 32

FIRST FLIGHT

December 1949

It was the second Saturday after Thanksgiving that my father woke me up on a cold crisp December morning at 6:00 AM. He was keeping a forgotten promise he made to me, and he had enlisted an accomplice to help fulfill my wildest dream.

He had gathered all my necessary clothing for the day's adventure, and he helped me to get quietly dressed in order not to wake the sleeping family. He had an extra set of winter mittens and a selection of scarves, hats, and winter leggings. I was quite curious why I would need all these extra outer garments, but his finger to his lips kept me quiet. We did not have breakfast, but instead left the home with as little noise as possible and exited the house through the rear pantry door instead of the front entrance. We walked down the walk way, and I started to turn right where I knew my father kept his truck in a neighbors garage, but he pulled me to the left down the brick side walk.

I asked, "Daddy, where are we going?"

He just smiled. "You'll see…be patient."

As we turned the corner of the street, I spotted a black late model Buick sedan with its engine bellowing out white puffs of vapor as it sat idling while parked at the curb. It was my godfather, Smithy who with a laugh in his voice exited the car as we approached him.

He had been my father's friend from childhood and always seemed to be in a good mood.

He asked my father, "Any trouble sneaking out of the house?"

My father greeted his laughing old friend with a nod of no and a quick handshake while telling him, "Let's get out of here before Josie finds us gone." The Josie he referred to was my mother named Josephine.

The two friends had hatched a plan that my father did not want my mother to know about, and it obviously included my participation to launch this devious plan.

My head was filled with so many questions as I stammered to my father, "Daddy...Daddy...What are we doing?"

He just laughed and picked me up, and we entered the front passenger seat with me sitting on his lap. "Oh, you're going to be so pleased with today, but first we need to eat, we have a long ride ahead of us."

Smithy quickly accelerated from the curb, and we began the unknown adventure. We had a long way to ride? Where are we going? What are we doing? Why all the secrets and the quiet departure from the house? There were too many questions for me to figure in my mind, so I decided to just let the day unfold and have its secrets revealed in the playing out of the day.

Smithy drove very fast as the early Saturday morning was devoid of most traffic, and he talked nonstop to my father as he bragged of the wheels he had set in motion for my big surprising adventure. He was very animated in his description of the skill and cunning that was required for him to display in order to fill his promise to my dad. He was very pleased with his efforts, and my father had to thank him over and over as Smithy kept urging my father's admiration for him.

We arrived at a diner about twenty minutes from our home, and Smithy finally stopped talking as we entered the diner. The diner was filled with truck drivers and construction men, and we walked to a corner booth to sit. The diner had an appetizing aroma of bacon and eggs cooking on the open grill, and I immediately felt a need to eat. We were fumbling through the greased-stained worn menus when a young attractive waitress walked over to our booth.

"What will you three men be eating this morning?" She winked at me when she asked the question. Smithy and my father both laughed with Smithy pointed his finger at me and telling her, "Better ask the young man direct. He can speak for himself."

I was so pleased to feel a part of the group and not just a ward of my father. It was the very early beginnings of my search for an identity and independence.

I proudly proclaimed, "I'll have bacon and eggs over easy with toast and orange juice."

She smiled a beautiful smile back at me. "Do you want coffee with that, sir?"

I looked for my father's help, but he told me to answer the waitress. I felt a blush over my face, but blurted out... "No, I want a hot chocolate with whipped cream on top."

Her beautiful smile returned, and I received a pat on my head from her for my efforts; I was in love, totally smitten with this young beautiful waitress. She took my father's and Smithy's same order of bacon and eggs, but with coffee instead of the hot chocolate and told us that she would be back in five minutes with our orders.

Smithy laughed and told my father that I was a chip off the old block. I also had a way with the ladies.

My father gave a sign with a waving of his hand that the subject of his "way with the ladies" was not to be discussed in front of his youngest son, but he did have a smile on his face when Smithy made the comment.

The waitress was true to her words and promptly arrived back with our meals in five minutes. I was starving and the food disappeared from my plate in two minutes with me and my father having to wait for the much slower eater Smithy to finish his bacon and eggs.

My hot chocolate was as advertised, piping hot, and while we were waiting for Smithy my father order two coffees to go and asked her to put my drink into a paper cup to go.

My father grew impatient with Smithy as he began to wipe his plate with a small piece of toast.

"Jesus. Smithy, when's the last time you've eaten?"

Smithy laughed out loud. "I ate at home right before I picked you two up."

My father abruptly stood up as the waitress returned with the beverages to go, handed her some cash while asking her if it would cover the bill and her tip. Her eyes opened wide as it was obvious that he indeed had given her a very good tip. A few "thank you very much" followed by another smile while patting my head had us leaving the diner and continuing the trip to an unknown destination.

We reentered the Buick and continued toward my unknown promised secret surprise. We began to drive in areas that I had never seen, and I questioned my father on what road we were driving that had us driving along the coast north of Boston.

"You'll see when we get there, little man, but to answer your question, we're on Route 1 north. Does that help you figure out where we're going?"

It meant nothing to my six-year-old mind, but it made me feel a part of the surprise before it was revealed to me. The ride seemed endless as we drove up the coast and passed through several small towns scattered around the Massachusetts coast. My father and Smithy made a lot of remarks about the strange landscapes, and it was apparent to me that they were most familiar with the route were traveling toward our destination.

At last Smithy told me, "It won't be long now, Butch."

I searched the roadside for any clue to our destination, but nothing registered in my limited travelled mind of the sights stretched out before me. Large wind swept sand dunes, tall reed like cat and nine tails, multiple unknown flowers with residues of their dead brown flowers still clinging to their stems and a landscape that was completely foreign to my eyes. I recognized the ocean and beach areas, but it was not any that I had ever played on during the summer months and the beaches had a harsh unwelcoming appearance as if to warn swimmers to beware of entering my waters.

There was a steady brisk wind coming off the ocean, and I heard my father ask Smithy if it would be safe in this wind. He quickly assured him that "Gus" was a professional and would not endanger me in any way.

"Endanger me"? What could that mean? I was soon to have all my questions answered.

It spread before me as a dream world of nature and of man's attempt of blending the harshness of asphalt and grass to form a small private airport at Plum Island, Massachusetts. There were WWII Quonset huts scattered along the short grass landing strip and several maintenance workshop buildings. A few small tailed wheel private aircraft were tied to their moorings and were being buffeted against their ropes with the brisk winds. An orange directional wind sock was blowing straight out in the direction of the sea breeze and varied its tail direction as the winds shifted in a flow of different directions.

My father broke the silence. "Smithy, where's Gus?"

Smithy pointed to a tiny orange dot in the sky coming to the airport. "There he is…that's him coming in for a landing."

Gus was coming into a landing in an orange yellow airplane. Who and what was Gus?

I couldn't take my eyes off the little orange yellow plane as it bounced along the sky. It appeared to be motionless and just floating in the air, but as it got closer to the grass runway, the forward speed of the aircraft became apparent. The aircraft started to fly in a crooked manner, and Smithy excitedly yelled, "Look at that slip. He's doing that to keep the plane lined up with the runway and to lose altitude."

At the very last moment before touchdown, the craft straightened out and landed on its front two wheels followed by its tail dropping to the grass strip.

Smithy let out a yell that startled me and my father who had been very quiet while observing the movement of the small craft.

Smithy ran to the now stopped aircraft screaming, "Come on. Come on!"

The aircraft's propeller came to a stop as we approached it, and Smithy helped the pilot exit the cockpit. When he stood next to Smithy, he appeared almost childlike in his stature. Gus was five foot nothing, and he had a shocking full head of pure white hair.

Gus Marino, a friend of Smithy, had been a P38 Army Air Corp flight instructor that had seen combat action in the Pacific during the waning days of WWII. He walked toward me and my father dressed in an army-issued flight suit stained with a variety of grease and oil stains. He was a seasonal crop dust pilot spraying potatoes in Maine who also had a flight school at the Plum Island Airport.

His face had a cartoonish feature of almost exploding when his face seemed to expand beyond natural limits when he smiled. It was impossible not to smile back at him in response to any of his facial expressions or at the sound of his rather high off-pitch way of speaking.

His accent easily made it clear that Gus was not from the local area, but he most definitely was Italian as his features had a southern Italian or Sicilian map printed on his face. He had rapid almost bird-like movements which only exaggerated his short stature. He was not what I would imagine any pilot to look like, but he was flying that yellow bird.

So this was my surprise; a visit to a real airport and to see up close, a small orange yellow airplane?

Gus came over to me and asked, "Are you ready, little guy?"

Ready? Ready...for what? My father pulled Smithy aside, and he had a looked of potential doom on his face. Smith quickly tried to calm my father's fear, "Don't worry, Andrew...Gus is an old pro...If it's not safe for Butch, he won't fly."

"Not safe for, Butch"...Did I hear him correctly? Why was I in danger?

It hit me like a bolt of lightning as I put it all together and realized that my surprise was just not coming to the airport, but to fly in the sky with the diminutive Gus Marino in his little yellow plane. I could hardly catch my breath, and I became so excited that my father placed his hand on my shoulder to keep me from jumping up and down as a frog in anticipation of my dream coming true.

Gus walked over to Dad and talked in a calmer manner then when we first met, and he assured him that it was very safe and not a danger to fly with this wind. Dad shook his hand while putting his arm around his short frame as if to give his approval, but at the same time to enforce his right of fatherhood when it came to decisions regarding my safety.

He was placing my life in Gus's hands, and he made Gus aware that it meant not to do anything foolish to jeopardize my well-being. They shook hands again, walked over to me, and we all started to walk toward the little plane with a grinning Smithy walking in trail behind us.

The bright sun was directly hitting the aircraft, and the bright color seemed to glow as it reflected the sunlight. Dad made a comment to Gus, as we approached closer to the craft, on how small it appeared and of the very small size of the engine's cylinder heads protruding from the nose of the plane.

Gus proceeded to speak in an excited animated speech about the safeness and capability of his pride and joy.

"This is a Piper J3 Cub...It's four years old with about 600 hours of flight time on its engine and airframe. The engine is a very reliable four cylinder 60 horse power air cooled, and I maintain it myself."

Dad looked stunned. "Sixty horse power? That's not much... How much does the plane weigh?"

Gus seemed a little put off by Dad's question, but his answers reassured him that I would be in good hands with him in his yellow bird. I had begun to worry that Dad would squelch the flight, but after Smithy explained a little more to him it was time to get the "show on the road" as Smithy shouted out. Dad came beside me and knelt to my height, "Butch, you okay with this flying business?"

My smile and body language answered his question; he turned to Gus. "Okay, Gus, take him up...that's my promise to him."

"Take me up!" I could not believe my ears; I was going to fly in a real airplane. Dad came over to me and asked me a rather practical question, "Do you have to pee? You better do it before you piss your pants in the sky."

This was followed by laughter from the three men, and Gus indicated to me that it was okay to just piss beside the plane sitting on the grass.

My very first official preflight action was to pee, not what I would consider a pilot's normal course of action, but this habit of urinating prior to entering any cockpit developed into a lifelong preflight event, and it took on an added importance as my ability to hold water diminished as I aged.

Gus showed me the fundamentals of the brief preflight actions on the J3 Cub, moving the flight control to make sure they moved freely, checking their connection to the control cables, draining fuel for any chance of water in the tank, checking visually the fuel level, engine oil level, and then he grabbed my hand to walk us behind the plane a fairly good distance in order for us to get a view of the entire bird.

He looked at the aircraft then spoke to me. "Remember to always do this as the last thing of your preflight. You'll be amazed how you will see things that are not correct by just seeing how the plane sits on the ground. You can spot a flat tire, dings in the airframe, loose skin fabric that you could miss by being too close to the plane. I guess it's like seeing the forest through the trees."

This advice has saved my ass on more than a few occasions, a rudder gust lock not removed, a bent up tail skid on a Boeing 757 not reported by the landing crew, flat spots on tires, and all sorts of oil and fuel leaks.

We walked to the front of the plane where Dad and Smithy were standing while Smithy was telling him about the little ship. Gus reached into the rear seat and pulled out two leather helmets with rubber hoses connected to imbedded earpieces in the helmets. This was to be our way of communicating amongst ourselves once we were seated into the craft. I reached out and touch the helmets. "Which one is mine?"

Gus handed me one of the helmets. "Let's see if this one fits."

Gus walked me to the entrance of the plane and lifted me into the front seat, which greatly surprised my father. He asked Gus how he was going to pilot from the rear seat.

Gus explained to Dad's satisfaction about keeping the aircraft in balance and that he needed to keep the lighter person up front. "Don't worry...I fly from the rear seat when I'm solo in it."

Gus had several seat cushions, and he adjusted them for me to sit on one and the other he squeezed behind my back. He tightened the seat belt and shoulder restraints tightly and gave them a tug to test them. "That should hold you in…Don't want you falling out of the plane."

Dad looked horrified when he said this, and Smithy laughed at him. "Andrew…he's only kidding. The plane has a door…see…He can't fall out."

The last task was to place the leather helmet on my head and to straighten out the rubber hoses that were connected to both helmets. The helmet fit perfectly, and Dad remarked that I had a big squash for my age.

Smithy defended me, "His head is big to fit all his brains. Don't worry he'll grow into his head."

Gus squeezed into the backseat, adjusted his helmet while checking our earpiece connection, and told Smithy to pull the prop through a few turns.

Smithy pulled the small prop easily in a circle with one hand, and my father looked surprised at his ease and knowledge of what Gus asked him to perform. It was obvious that Smithy had flown with Gus on other occasions.

Gus barked out from the rear seat, and Smithy responded on his actions and commands.

"Smithy…Ignition on."

"Roger…Mags are hot."

"Standby to rotate the prop."

"Roger on the prop."

A thumbs-up by Gus and Smithy prop kicked-started the little engine to life. A few throttle movements by Gus and the engine had a smooth loud nonmuffled sound.

I was beside myself with the anticipation of actually being in this plane that was going to take me into the sky. I had trouble controlling my body and squirmed in my seat to see in all directions. Gus told me to stop squirming; he had adjusted the restraints with me facing forward in my seat. I immediately stopped, and I began to look at the cockpit and saw that it had a "wet compass" attached above the small instrument panel. There were several gauges on the panel, which were probably associated with the engine, and I saw a dial that obviously was an altimeter as it was stamped inside with the word *altimeter*. I looked down at my feet, which were a good height above the rudder pedals, and I saw the constant movement of the pedals as Gus was "S" turning while he taxied the aircraft down the grass strip to the takeoff end.

I jumped as I heard Gus's voice come into my ears. "Butch, can you hear me? Raise your right hand if you hear me." I did as he instructed, and I was thrilled to hear his voice over the sound of the engine. We continued to taxi, and at the end of the grass strip runway, Gus sharply pivoted to the left to reverse the aircraft into a takeoff position on the runway.

He warned me that the ride would be bumpy at first, but that it would get smoother as we climbed higher into the sky. I just could not believe the words I was hearing, "Climbing higher into the sky."

This was really happening. I was not dreaming. I was wide awake to have my first flight into the sky.

"Are you ready for takeoff?"

I raised my right hand.

"Okay…Here we go!"

The engine roared to full power, and the Cub began to roll forward as Gus seemed to be moving all the controls at once, and as we accelerated, he pushed slight forward stick to raise the tail off the ground. He was working the rudder pedals to maintain directional control as we rolled down the grass strip. I was too small to see over the instrument panel, and I could only see above the aircraft and down at the grass runway. As we went faster, Gus moved the control stick to a mid-level neutral position quickly followed by a slight pull back on the control stick.

We lifted off the ground, and I could now see forward in front of the airplane. We were flying; I was stunned by the sudden leap into the air, but soon became aware of the turbulence as the small plane started to get buffeted by the gusty surface winds. My stomach was going from updrafts to down drafts, and I was getting thrown sideways in my seat. I became a little anxious until I heard from Gus. "Hang in there, Butch…just a little higher and it will get smooth." Like magic as soon as he finished talking, we were sailing not flying smoothly through the cold crisp air. It was incredible for my senses to take in the sounds, sights, and the pressures on my body as we continue to climb higher and higher.

It was exactly as I dreamed in my sleep of how the sky and ground would appear while flying, but the feel of the pressures on my body from the turns and the wind was not anticipated by me, and it took me a few minutes to adjust to the "feel" of flying.

After a few minutes, I was able to relax and take in all the wonderful sights as we continued to climb to about 3,000 feet. Gus continuously asked me how I was doing, and I had to repeatedly raise my right hand to acknowledge his inquiries to my well-being.

We were aloft for about ten minutes, and Gus headed out to the nearby coastline and flew north around the Cape Ann area of Massachusetts. He began a shallow descent, but there was no turbulence associated with the lower altitude while Gus guided our flight north along the coast's shore line. We were flying following the contours of the coast and the gentle rolling of the wings left and right heightened the sense of being in the sky.

Gus pointed out a few landmarks along the coast, but my eyes were taking in the sky and looking more at the horizon. Gus promised that I would be flying the craft in a few minutes, which caused me to almost lose my breath over his words.

Gus was continuing to fly up the coast as he split the waterline right down the middle of the Cub. Our left wing was over the sandy beach and our right wing was over the sudsy surf of the ocean's water. Gus suddenly added full power to the Cub, and he initiated a climb to a much higher altitude. I could see far off buildings south of our position, and Gus pointed out the distant Boston skyline with the original John Hancock Insurance Company's structure being the only tall building in its sky line.

He pointed out the Merrimack River and how it weaved through the various mill towns of Lawrence and Lowell, Massachusetts. He pointed to the towns of Amesbury and Newburyport where my father's families had settled after arriving in America.

Gus leveled the plane at 5,000 feet and told me to make sure that my seat belt was still tight around my body as he was going to do a little "air work."

He assured me that it would be nice and easy as I continued to take in the now greater viewing areas. There wasn't a cloud in the December morning sky and the brightness of the blue sky and the rising sun had me squinting as the brightness hurt my eyes.

Gus instructed me to put my hands on the control stick that ran up the middle of the cockpit and to feel how it moved when he did the air work from the rear seat.

Gus said, "Are you ready?"

My right hand went up, and he announced that we were going to do a gentle "lazy eight," which was a maneuver of a gradual turning climb to about a 90 degrees heading change with a descent to the original altitude until you were 180 degrees from the original heading at your starting altitude and then a reversal back to the original heading as you scribed the figure eight along the horizon. It was a climb and descent of 500 feet during the performance of the maneuver.

As I held the stick, I could feel the control pressures and a slight vibration from the controls surfaces connected to the stick by the control cables. The stick felt alive in my small hands, and I was eager to see if I could duplicate the maneuver. I was aware of the rudder moving as Gus turned the aircraft as they are used in conjunction with the stick to make a "coordinated" turn, but when Gus told me to try to fly the aircraft, he explained how he would help with the rudder pedals as my feet could not reach them.

I grabbed the control stick with both hands and under Gus's instructions began to try to duplicate what Gus had just shown me. I had difficulty on moving the control stick to its full range of motion as Gus had me cinched down so tightly in my seat, but I could feel his hands correcting my attempt of flying the yellow bird.

He was quite pleased with my initial efforts, and as I felt him take control of the plane, I released my grip on the stick. He told me to just sit back into my seat as he was going to do some other air work.

Chandelles, more figure eights, wingovers, a series of wing stalls, and he finished off with a hammerhead stall. The hammerhead had my stomach turning as we hesitated at the top of the vertical nose up position then sliding slightly back on its tail before Gus kicked hard right rudder, and we ended with the nose of the plane pointing straight down toward the ground.

The position of nose up to nose down, zero airspeed to maximum airspeed in a very rapid exchange of positions caused a quick roller coaster effect on my stomach, but I loved it.

Gus's remark of how I was doing great and that I showed no signs of getting airsick had me beaming with pride.

"You're doing great, little man!"

He once again told me to grab the controls while pointing to a point east of the coast and had me turn the airplane in its direction. We were headed back to the Plum Island Airport.

A series of turn and stop turning instructions by Gus brought the airport in sight in about ten minutes as Gus reduced the power to begin a descent for landing. He guided my nose angle during the descent as he made gradual small input changes to the engine throttle control until he brought the engine back to its idle position.

During the descent, he explained two instruments showing on my instrument panel—an airspeed indicator and the altimeter.

The airspeed indicator was a simple round dial with a needle pointing at your indicated airspeed and the altimeter was another dial that had needles rotating around numbers printed around its dial.

They were simple to read and their interpretation was simple enough that when Gus asked me my airspeed and altitude I quickly gave the correct answers.

My aptitude of understanding these basic readings impressed Gus as he stated, "Very good...can't be stupid and be a good pilot."

When we got below 1,500 feet the little yellow bird really started to fishtail and wing waggle, causing me to overcorrect the control inputs.

Gus remarked, "Easy partner...nice and easy...treat her like a lady." That was the first reference to "her" for an airplane and the first in person use of "partner" I ever heard. The ground loomed closer and closer, and Gus took complete control of the plane to line up for the final landing.

We entered overhead the airport, and Gus made a series of turns before he had us lined up on the final leg facing the runway. He had me once again grab the controls and wanted me to go through the landing with him. I watched and felt the controls rapid short movements and was most aware of the constant rudder displacement as the wind began to whip up in intensity and vary its direction as we got lower and lower.

I could judge that our angle would not put us at the end of the runway, but too far down the runway when Gus crossed controlled the inputs to the aircraft. He held the stick full left and he stepped on the rudder full right to cause a forward "slip" that greatly increase the sink rate and had us maintaining a ground path that kept us lined up with the runway.

Gus timed it perfectly, and he adjusted our altitude to touch down about 100 feet from the runway's threshold. He struggled to keep the plane tracking down the center of the runway as the wind was now mostly blowing off our left, trying to drift us to the right and "weather cocking" the nose of the plane to the left.

We touched down first on the left main gear tire quickly following up with the right main gear tire and a few seconds later the tail wheel touched down onto the grass strip. Gus slammed on the rudder pedal heel brakes and the aircraft came to an abrupt stop after a few hundred feet.

My first flight was over; the one hour flight seemed like five minutes.

I did not want to become a pilot; I needed to be a pilot! Want had been replaced by need.

Gus taxied the Cub toward the aircraft tie down area and pointed out my father and Smithy as we got closer to our original taxi point. Smithy was in a constant state of movement while Dad seemed frozen to one spot on the grass apron area.

Gus "gunned" a quick burst of the throttle to turn the plane into a 180 degree turn by using a hard left rudder and locking the left brake. He simultaneously pulled the fuel lever on the engine and we spun into the opposite direction with the engine stopped.

I sat in the tiny cockpit trying to grasp the reality of actually being in the sky with Gus. It had registered as a live dream in my mind, and I was unable to bring the event into a more conscious level of reality. It did no matter; I knew it was real, and my mind would just have to catch up with my emotions.

Smithy came running toward the plane skipping and shouting while clapping his hands over his head. He had a huge grin from ear to ear and his excited words were not heard by me as my helmet and earphones completely muffled his words.

Dad walked unhurriedly in our direction with a pensive expression fixed on his face with his left hand in his pants pocket and a cigarette in his right fingers.

Gus helped me from the Cub and removed the leather helmet that was beginning to annoy me and gave me a huge grin and a quick thumbs-up "Okay."

As my dad got closer, Gus told him that I had a good natural feel for flying and showed no fear or any hint of air sickness.

"Butch is a natural!" These words from Gus further fueled my need to be a pilot—I was a natural.

I jumped up onto my father, and he picked me up into his arms; he gave me a hard protective hug and smiled as he spoke to me.

"Well, little man...you got your promised wish...You'll never forget today...never."

My father always seemed aware of the passage of time and how fleeting your life could be as you aged; he liked giving us memories in order to have a sense of control of this passage of time.

Gus made a comment to Dad that I should take flying lessons in my early teens if I wanted to be a professional pilot; Dad's expression said otherwise. There would be no flight lessons in my immediate future.

The temperature was dropping rapidly, and the men were anxious to get into their cars for warmth and to begin the ride to their homes.

Smithy helped Gus tie down the Cub while my dad started up Smithy's Buick. Gus jumped into his Studebaker pickup truck with unknown faded writing on the driver's door, and we heard the crank-ing and the putt putt as the engine was trying to fire all its cylinders.

Gus walked over to me with an extended hand, but I reached up to him and surprised him with a hug. He smiled his cartoon-ish grin while patting my head and then walked over to shake my father's hand. A few thank-yous were exchange and a quick punch to Smithy's shoulder and off Gus went in his pickup truck bouncing down the dirt road.

Dad rubbed his cold hands together and gave this rendition in Italian, "Andiamo ci, a la casa…Let's go home."

The day of my first flight was to be the last for a long time.

CHAPTER 33

FLIGHT 996

I was woken by a noise from the front galley, and when I checked my watch, it was only about five minutes before one of the FA was supposed to wake me to resume my duties in the cockpit. I stretched from my uncomfortable sleeping position and visited the Blue Room with my ditty bag where I did my ritual of brushing my teeth, washing my face, and try to make it look like I just didn't wake up. I reflected on my dream as it brought a mix of smiles and a feeling of sadness thinking that they were all gone except me. Gone, but remembered by me until I no longer was on the right side of the ground or God forbid, unable to remember that day.

The smell of fresh brewed coffee had me step behind a curtain into the galley area. An ebony-faced African American FA named Lydia was preparing some snacks while brewing fresh coffee. I stood with her waiting for the coffee to finish brewing while just enjoying to look at Lydia.

She was drop-dead gorgeous, twenty-three years old at the most, tall with a body that most women envied and men lusted over. She caught me looking at her and flashed her brilliant white teeth while smiling at me.

"Get you anything, Captain?"

"Just waiting for the coffee and enjoying the view."

Lydia called me toward her by waving her finger to come closer to her; she whispered to me, "Now...you didn't hear this from me...

Mary is upset tonight because she is nervous waiting for a biopsy report on a lump in her breast."

Mary's irregular behavior was now explained, but I was a little angry with her for not telling me and for her also coming to work with the stress of worrying about the biopsy.

Lydia continued to talk, "Mary is quite upset and afraid that you're angry with her...You know how we all like flying with Captain Smiley."

"Are you trying to butter up the old captain?"

She grabbed my face and gave my cheek a slight pinch with a soft affectionate slap and with the coffee pot in her hand proceeded down the aisle of the aircraft. I marveled at the sight of her sensuous body movement. *Whoa, old man...Calm yourself...Those days are long gone.*

I made a mental note to talk to Mary, but I was eager to get into the cockpit to check on our flight status. Joe was sitting in my left seat and Frank was in the first officer's seat. We played musical chairs, and I ended up in the left seat, Joe in the right seat, and Frank in the middle jump seat.

I glanced at the information displayed on the glass computer flight indicators and asked Joe for an update.

"Skipper, we're on schedule, 3,000 pounds up on the fuel, try-ing to talk to Scottish Control to get further clearance. Weather at London Heathrow Airport...2,500 broken, visibility eight miles, winds 320 degrees at 25 knots gusting to 35 with lower level chop and potential wind shear advisory in affect." We briefed the current approach and arrival procedure in use at Heathrow, and I sat back drinking my coffee. I saw that we were approaching our clearance limit point and prodded Frank to get Scottish Control on the HF to get our clearance into the airspace.

I made a call into the cabin expecting to brief Mary, but Lydia had assumed lead FA at Mary's request, so I relayed all the informa-tion she needed to prep the cabin for the approach and landing in London.

While Lydia's voice was trailing off the intercom, a loud unin-telligible screeching voice came over the Scottish Control HF frequency. The only recognizable word was "United 996," and we looked at each other and said the same thing, "What the hell did he just say?"

I started to laugh when the same squealing and heavily accented Indian/English voice again attempted to give instructions to UAL 996.

"Any of you getting what he's saying?"

"Not me, Skipper" came from Joe and Frank.

I grabbed the hand mic and told Scottish control, "Say again."

Same voice came back at us again with the same results.

With an edge to my voice, I said, "Scottish Control, UAL 996 unable to understand. Have you 5 by 5, but unable to understand the words."

The "fun" was about to begin.

The Scottish Control Center obviously had Indian nationals working their radios and because of their heavy Indian accents, speech patterns and rapidity of speech were very difficult to understand over the airwaves. My patience was zero when dealing with this situation and the following incident will perhaps help explain my impatience.

United had a few Pakistani First Officers on the B-767 and how they ever were considered to be English proficient for their FAA pilot certificates was a mystery to most who had the misfortune to have them in their cockpit.

I have to admit that I am not the most patient captain when it comes to me exercising my duties as the captain of the flight crew, but you properly figured that out by now from some of my rantings in my writings.

This first officer's English was so bad that I could not understand him in the cockpit, and when he talked on the radios, I had to clarify every one of his communications that he transmitted. I gave him the facts, "What comes out of your mouth is not English…It is unintelligible gibberish."

This set him off as he took it as an insult of his perceived knowledge of speaking English and considering their culture probably to his entire family. The angrier he got, the less I could understand him, but he made a big mistake when he flashed his temper by throwing a half-filled coffee cup onto the floor.

My wife tells me that when I get really angry, I should look in the mirror to see my bulging eyes, red face, and veins popping out of my neck and temple while I scream and spit at the same time.

Well this unfortunate first officer was the beneficiary of this wonderful sight as I screamed for him to push his seat back from the controls and just "Shut the Christ up!"

His demeanor quickly changed. "Ah, but too late…No second chances by me in my workplace…none."

I handle the duties of flying the aircraft and talking to the various controllers, and it went this way until we touched down in KLGA. I would not even let him read the checklist, but read it aloud to myself to get it on tape. He just stared out the cockpit window unsure of what to do if anything to smooth over this situation that could mean his termination at United Airlines.

I parked the aircraft and told him to stay seated; he meekly complied.

I had an old friend who was fleet captain on the B-767 and head of their training at the center in Denver. My solution was to call him and have them evaluate not only his English proficiency, but his piloting ability as he did not handle the flight controls on this trip for me to evaluate.

This could save his job, for if I had told what had happened on the flight, he probably would have been fired or at least removed from flight status for a review of his training records.

I told him what I was going to recommend to my friend, and he did not protest. I guess my reactions to his little tantrum and his lack of English proficiency made him realize the seriousness of his situation.

I got up out of my seat and grabbed my flight bag while he sat in his seat. I was very thankful that this was the last leg of my scheduled trips and the only reason he was on board was his status as a reserved pilot based in LA.

I would never see this pilot again, and my friend took my suggestion very seriously with the FO being pulled back for additional evaluation and training. I never found out what happened to him nor did I really care; you don't belong in my cockpit if you're incompetent.

The Scottish controller attempted to again communicate his instruction to us with the same results. This was going to take tact and diplomacy. I caught a look at Joe's face with his slight smile as if he knew what was going to happen.

"Scottish Control…United 996 request a change of controller. Unable to understand current controller."

This resulted in the same controller getting angry, talking faster and of course less intelligible.

I looked at our position and realized we needed to get further flight clearance down our route or we'd be force to hold at our current clearance limit. I was getting irritated, and I suppose it showed as Joe warned Frank, "You better cover your ears…This is going to get ugly."

Joe had seen me explode at a "Rampy" in LAX; it was ugly.

I bellowed over the radio, "Scottish Control looking for further flight clearance."

Same controller, same results; I asked for his super to get on the horn.

No answer.

With as much control as I could muster, I screamed over the radio, "Get me a new controller or I will declare an emergency and come in unannounced with no clearance into Heathrow due to emergency fuel status and loss of communications!"

The next voice from Scottish Control was very upper-class Queen's English with a controlled manner of speaking to emphasize the professional difference in my obviously annoyed manner of speaking.

I was not going to let them get one up on me or my crew and stated, "Scottish Control, I know that Scotland is an isolated rock situated in the cold North Atlantic Ocean, but surely you can find more qualified personnel willing to suck it up for the queen and man your radios."

A moment later…"United 996, cleared as filed…expect such and such approach…contact on frequency…etc., etc.…Bye bye."

"Bye bye," a term that was used by the Brits in ending their radio communications.

I replied, "Roger, Scottish Control…Bye bye…Cheers…Stiff upper lip…Jolly good show," and every other idiotic British expression I could remember, which caused Joe and Frank to laugh.

Joe looked at me and I barked, "Fuck you…You're as useless as teats on a boar hog!"

We all started to laugh out loud and Joe stated, "Another example of a tactful handling of a situation demonstrated by Captain Angelo."

This prompted me to punch Joe in his left arm, and he proceeded to initiate his best impression of mock agony.

At moments like this as a captain, I could not imagine my life without the infusion of the entire good and bad of my profession; these moments I would miss the most.

We worked the flight through the standard "chain of command" centers and approach control until we had descended down to our initial approach altitude based on transmission commands and depicted chart profiles. I called the cabin and issued instructions to button it up and to prepare the cabin for the approach and landing at Heathrow Airport. I gave my standard briefing to the passengers over the PA system, and we did our mandatory arrival and approach brief in the cockpit.

I reminded Joe and Frank, "Let's not forget to reset the altimeter to the airport field setting at the broadcasted transition altitude."

This is different than in the USA where we go from a standard pressure altitude setting of 29.92 inches set in our altimeter and change to local altimeter settings at 18,000 feet.

In Europe and most of the world, you can change at a much lower altitude that is broadcasted over the airport information, ATIS and is called Transition Altitude or Transition Level depending if you were climbing or descending.

On a previous flight, we had neglected to change to the field altimeter setting, and we were politely advised by the British Controllers, "Please check your altitude."

The British always seemed to be in complete control, but I wondered how cool they would be in the traffic density areas of KLGA, KEWR and KJFK when the weather turned bad and the jets were stacked at different points and altitudes waiting their turn for the approach and landing.

The communications were so jammed that the controllers would declare, "No read back," which meant to eliminate the required read back of their instructions and to initiate what they told you to do.

The British Controllers were very cool and professional, but I knew our controllers were the best in the world. Most of the controllers in the Golden Triangle between Boston, New York City, and Washington DC had local accents and manner of speaking, which was absolutely necessary in order for them to talk in that necessary rapid fast pace staccato cadence of the Northeastern USA.

When I had a new first officer, especially one from the South, I often had to have them fly the airplane as they could not listen or talk fast enough for the controllers. If you screwed up their instructions, they would vector you out of the traffic flow as a punishment to "spin" for about fifteen minutes in a "holding pattern."

The transition from initial approach to the final vectoring for the landing went as advertised, and we received the updated airport weather conditions. The winds were now at 320 degrees variable to 360 degrees at 35 knots gusting to 45 knots with wind shear advisories in effect. Frank remarked, "Jesus, it's a freaking hurricane!"

I no sooner briefed the FA and passengers that it would be turbulent on landing when we were hit with some light to moderate "chop."

I added my maximum wind and gust factor of 20 knots and, we had a "target approach speed" of about 150 knots determined by our flap setting and landing weight. This speed was set on a grommet called a bug on the dial of the airspeed indicator and it was called a "Bug in Bug out" approach speed, which meant that you referenced this speed until the final touch down segment or you referenced this speed on a missed approach to the landing as a "Go around speed."

I cinched my restraints tighter than normal and told my guys, "Get ready for a rough ride, keep your eyes open for traffic, and call out if I'm screwing up."

The approach checklist, approach and landing briefing were completed, and we were descending via approach controls instructions for the approach to ILS runway 27L at Heathrow Airport.

The descent was bronco busting rough, and we were getting thrashed around with the chop, which caused a fluctuation in our vertical descent rate as well as having the airspeed indicator needle wildly fluctuating. I knew that the lowering of the landing gear with its pendulum affect would help calm the ride, and Joe was nervously hovering near the gear handle to wait for my command to lower the gear.

I smiled at him. "Joe, ya think we should probably slow up and get some flaps out before we drop the gear?"

He said nothing and now his hand was rested on the flap extension handle as the turbulence intensity increased to a very uncomfortable level. Frank made a remark that the passengers must be really getting banged around and his voiced reflected the strain on his own body.

The ride was getting my adrenaline flowing as my body and mind responded with a heightened increase in rapid eye movements as I scanned the instruments with quicker reflex responses to the control yoke and displacements of the plane's control surfaces.

I kept the speed between 220 and 240 knots indicated with a clean configuration—flaps up, gear up, and I adjusted the sink rate and airspeed by using the speed brakes to try to keep the twin engine turbofans spooled up for a quicker response to their inputs.

Joe saw what I was doing and told Frank to standby for a Navy Carrier Landing at Heathrow. I laughed at his remark and commented that the old man was earning his captain's pay on this landing.

I guided the B-767 from a base leg to a final approach, and we received our clearance for the ILS approach with the appropriate instruction on the tower frequency to contact.

As we turned on to the final leg to line up with the runway, our aircraft nose was about 45 degrees to the right of center in a crab to track the aircraft down the runway's center line.

I squealed, "Ride'm, cowboys," in anticipation of a test of my pilot's skills on this landing. My reflexes were a little slower than thirty years ago, but experience, anticipation with an extensive time in "type" allowed me to be in tune and in touch with the ship through my fingers while my subconscious mind made up for any loss of reflex speed.

I bragged to the guys, "Okay…Let the old man show you how a maximum cross wind landing is done." This also was a way to boost up my own confidence and not to screw up the landing.

I began to slow the aircraft with the speed brakes and called for approach flaps and landing gear at the same time. Joe quickly responded, "Roger, approach flaps…Gear down," as he accomplished my requests at the same time.

Seconds later…"Gear down…three green."

I now configured the craft to our full flap landing configuration as the glide path indicator of the ILS was about one dot high as we approached it from below the approximate 3 degrees glide angle, which would guide us to the proper runway target zone.

I was bracketing the target speed of 150 knots as the wind gusts were causing severe fluctuations in the indicated airspeed.

I was more or less in the groove, pumped to the max and loving every minute of the challenge. This was what I was born to do; no 9 to 5 job could equal the adrenaline rush of the excitement and responsibility of having 250 people's lives depend on my skills and "brass balls" to land them safely at their destination.

Joe and Frank were quiet, afraid to distract the old captain from his task at hand as I was talking out loud to myself on the procedures at hand.

"Watch your speed…Watch your sink rate…! More power, followed by less power…Watch the center line… correct your crab angle."

I was working all my hands and feet with rapid eye scans in and out of the cockpit to assure staying on center line and on the glide path.

The ship crossed the approach end of the runway with large fluctuations in the airspeed, descent rate, and my having to constantly adjust my crab angle to stay on center line. The actual touchdown would be critical to execute with precision.

I talked to myself, "Come on Butchie Boy…Let's impress all the passengers who are anticipating a slamming down hard landing on the runway and let's show your crew that the old guy still got it!"

At one hundred feet, I started to test the crab angle and to lower the right wing into the cross wind while applying left rudder to keep the aircraft from actually turning right. This was a forward slip from a crab to touch down with the drifting of the aircraft at zero with the nose of the aircraft pointing down the runway. This often had the aircraft touching down on the upwind main gear first quickly followed by the other downwind main gear.

The wind was fierce and unrelenting even as we got lower to the ground.

As the automatic radar altimeter altitudes were announced, I was pumped up and ready.

"Fifty feet…" Slight crab and increase of lowering of right wing.

"Thirty feet…" On airspeed…sink rate good…tracking down runway wing low and cross rudder.

"Twenty feet…" Check auto brakes level three.

At the twenty-foot announcement, I began to check my sink rate with a slight easy pull up on the yoke but kept my power at the same level. "Easy, sweetheart," came from my lips as the ship started to drift a little left. I threw in a slight crab to check the drift and started to ease back on the power.

The moment of truth, perfect timing, wing down, zero drift, tracking down the center line, minimum sink rate, on target speed and then the sweetest sound.

No squealing of the tires, but just the sound of the auto speed brake handle pulling back to deploy the ground speed brakes, which dumps the lift off the wings to allow for max braking with the auto brake landing system.

A genuine "grease job."

A lot of left rudder input to keep the aircraft from "weather cocking" into the wind while keeping it tracking down the center of the runway and into reverse thrust at the same time by lifting the throttle levers over the "gate" into full reverse.

In a matter of seconds, the ship slowed to allow nose wheel steering through the steering "tiller," and we quickly came out of reverse as Joe called out 80 knots and the speed brakes were stowed.

I taxied off the high speed taxi exit as instructed, and no one made a comment on the landing. I had impressed myself, but no comment from Joe or Frank.

Then Joe slapped my right shoulder and shouted, "Jesus Christ, Skipper, you lucked out on that landing!

I was about to say something about it being skill when they both agreed that the "old man" still got it. I acknowledged that indeed they were correct, but maybe my ass had helped...I did not want to bust it!

I wiped a slight trickle of sweat off my left cheek as it ran down from my temple; I was glad it was on my left side out of view lest my reputation of being captain cool be tainted.

We cleaned up the ship as we taxied and ran through our after landing checklist. Flaps up, speed brakes stowed, APU started, and the various after-landing cockpit flows confirmed by the checklist callouts.

I loved the sequential green lights on the ground at Heathrow that lead you right to your parking gate. I suddenly felt the effort of the landing and of the all night flight from KJFK, but I was still basking in my own sense of glory over the landing.

We secured the ship, and Frank opened the cockpit door. All comments from the passengers were on the roughness of the approach, but no comments on my great landing until a grizzly older gentleman of obvious elite British bearing inquired on who made the landing.

Joe and Frank pointed to me and the elder man stated that my landing was unbelievably smooth considering the wind conditions.

His next comment was straight out of a British movie, "Bloody good show!"

He gave me a smile and a thumbs-up sign while he continued to exit the aircraft.

Joe and Frank jumped out of the cockpit, and I looked back to see our FAs moving with lightning speed to leave. I gave Joe a one-minute wait for me to follow as I sat in my prized seat quickly reflecting on the night's flight.

I slowly left the aircraft with the ground personnel unloading the cargo bins and saw that the entire crew had entered the large bus to take us to a separate crew custom inspection site.

They were waving at me to hurry my joining them when the image from the film, *The High and the Mighty*, from a book by Ernie Gann came to mind.

At the end of the movie, the first officer played by John Wayne, who was older than the captain, was walking away from his aircraft after a harrowing flight from Hawaii to San Francisco. An old friend watched him walking away with a limp and as the character turned to wave goodbye his friend whispered to himself as he waved in return...

"Good night, you old pelican."

It suddenly dawned on me...I had become John Wayne's character.

I was now..."THE OLD PELICAN."

THE END

Appreciation and Thank You

I will begin with the obvious from my title, my father, Andrew J. Angelo. The hearing of my father's voice during the flight was very real, and this book is a reflection more of my emotions toward him than the facts surrounding him in the book.

Charlie Califf...I believe that if I were alone on that flight or with someone other than Charlie that the outcome may not have ended so well. He kept me focused on not being too anxious because of my concern of his well-being, and our bantering during the flight was a relief valve for the tension over our dire situation.

I wish to thank the entire flight crew of the Air Force C-130 aircraft and the entire flight crew of the Coast Guard ASR Helicopter from Cape Cod, Massachusetts, on their tremendous efforts that led to pointing the way to a safe descent through the dark overcast skies of New England.

Tremendous thanks to the entire FAA ATC system from Teterboro Airport, New York Center and of the entire team effort of the Boston ARTCC. Their professionalism with a tireless effort in coordinating the rescue aircrafts and ground facilities was the basis of our rescue.

I thank my mother, Josephine, who always wanted the best for me and expected the best from me. She gave me the endurance that was needed that November night.

I thank my big brother Joe, my sister Mary Ann, and my oldest brother Mario who I'm very sad will not get to read the story.

I send a special appreciation to my then-wife, Janet Cavagnaro Angelo, who endured the craziness and upset of being married to a military man and professional pilot.

A hug and a kiss to my then young kids, Michele and Andrew, whose existence tempered my efforts to survive that night.

A special thanks to Executive Flyers Aviation whose founder over fifty years ago, Myron "Mike" Goulian, paved the way for my position at Deckhouse. To the Goulian family, Rita "Diva" Goulian, Mike Jr, the airshow pilot and air race pilot and to Matt Goulian who has provide quite a few laughs for me.

This story would not have been put on paper or led me to write other books and movie scripts if it were not for my current wife, Roseanne Chiaraluce Angelo, to whom I told this story many years ago. Her insistence of me to put this to paper opened up an entirely new world to me within the writing community in many fields. It led to my involvement in movie scripts, which are in various stages of production and development as well as other books, *Winter Hill Dreams of Flight* and *Forever Love*.

Wings of My Father was originally written as a movie script and a rewriting based on this book is now in progress.

I would be remiss in not mentioning my youngest son, Christopher, and he would never forgive me. My stepchildren: John, Lisa, and Jeanine deserve a thank you for also enduring my some-times not so pleasant demeanor.

A very special thanks to John Conners and the guys at the Troupe Digital Media Production from Windham, New Hampshire. John has consistently assisted me in many of my endeavors of the last few years with his insights and encouragement of my efforts. He's been a great listener and has provided me with some rather colorful comical relief.

Thanks to Dr. Chris Sweeney and to his organization that has given me the years to accomplish my writings and to many future years.

To all that contributed to my aviation career and life, a special thanks…

ALPHABETICAL LIST
OF AERONAUTICAL
ABBREVIATIONS

A
A/C... aircraft
ACARS... aircraft communication and addressing reporting system
ACAS... airborne collision avoidance system
ACFT... aircraft
ADI... attitude director indicator
AFDS... autopilot flight director system
AGL...above ground level
ALS... approach lighting system
AMSL... above mean sea level
AP... autopilot
ASI... airspeed indicator
ATC... air traffic control
ATPL... airline transport pilot license
ATS... air traffic service

C
CAA... Civil Aviation Authority
CAS... calibrated airspeed
CDI... course deviation indicator

CDU... control/display unit
CFIT... controlled flight into terrain
CG... center of gravity
CPDLC... controller pilot data link communications
CTAF... common traffic advisory frequency
CTR... controlled traffic region/control zone
CVR... cockpit voice recorder

D
DA... density altitude
DER...departure end of the runway
DG... directional gyro
DR... dead reckoning

E
EFIS... electronic flight instrument system
EGPWS... enhanced ground proximity warning system
EPR... engine pressure ratio
ESA... emergency safe altitude
ETA... estimated time of arrival
ETD... estimated time of departure

F
FAA... Federal Aviation Administration
FAF... final approach fix
FAP... final approach point
FBO... fixed-base operator
FC... flight crew
FDR... flight data recorders (black box)
FL... flight level
FMA... flight mode annunciator
FMC...flight management computer
FMS... flight management system
F/O first officer
FA... flight attendant

FPA... flight path
FSS...flight service station

G

GA... general aviation
GA... go-around
GCA... ground control approach
GND... ground
GPU... ground power unit
G/S... glide slope
GS...ground speed

H

HDG... heading
HIRL... high intensity runway lightning
HLD... hold
HIS... horizontal situation indicator
HW... head wind
HYD... hydraulic

I

IAC... instrument approach chart
IAF... initial approach fix
IAP... instrument approach procedure
IAS... indicated airspeed.
ICO... idle cut off
IDT... transponder ident
IF... intermediate fix
IFP... instrument flight procedures
IFR... instrument flight rules
IMC... instrument meteorological conditions
ISA... international standard atmosphere

K

KIAS...knots indicated airspeed
KTAS... knots true airspeed

L/M

LW...landing weight
MAP... missed approach point
MEA... minimum en route altitude
MDA... minimum descent altitude
MOCA.... minimum obstruction clearance altitude
MSL... mean sea level

O

OAT... outside air temperature
OEI... one engine inoperative

P

PA... pressure altitude
PAPI... precision approach path indicator
PAR... precision approach radar
PAX... passenger
PET... point of equal time
PF... pilot flying
PFD... primary flight display
PFAF... precision final approach
PC... pilot in command
PIREP... pilot report
PM... pilot monitoring
PNF... pilot not flying
PNR... point of no return
PTT... push to talk

Q

QFE... atmospheric pressure at aerodrome elevation
QNH... altimeter subscale setting to obtain elevation when on the
ground (altitude above MSL)

R

RA... radio altitude or radar altimeter
RTO... rejected takeoff

RWY... runway
RW... ramp weight

S
SAR... surveillance approach radar
SID... standard instrument departure
SIGMET... significant meteorological Information
SOP... standard operational procedures
STAR... standard terminal arrival route

T
TAS... true airspeed
TDZ... touch down zone
TWR... tower
TWY... taxiway

U
UHF...ultra-high frequency (radio)
UTC...Universal Time Coordinated

V
VASI... visual approach slope indicator
VDP... visual descent point
VFR... visual flight rules
VHF... very high frequency (radio)
VMC... visual meteorological conditions
VSI... vertical speed indicator
V... Velocity

W
WS... wind shear
WTC... wake turbulence category
WX... weather

X
XMIT... transmit

XPDR... transponder or XPNDR

Y
Y... Yaw
Y/D yaw damper

Z
Z... Zulu time (UTC)
ZFT... zero fuel time
ZFW... zero fuel weight

My childhood home

My parents, Andrew and Joshephine Angelo

Pensacola preflight Cadet 1964

First flight J3CUB

Boston ATC November 15, 1971

Typical light Piper Twin Aircraft Cockpit

Example of a light twin aircraft

Entrance to Hanscom Air Base Civil Terminal

Original Terminal Building Nashua Airport

Entrance to Nashua Airport

Site of FAA celebration in hotel bar

Sign of FAA in Nashua, NH

ABOUT THE AUTHOR

Captain Andrew J. Angelo, UAL ret., had a distinguished professional aviation career as a naval flight officer and as an international airline captain with United Airlines. He served with the United States Navy during the Vietnam conflict and received commendations and medals for his participation in air combat missions. Captain Angelo has extensive experience in many fields of aviation and serves as an aviation consultant in a prestigious DC-based consulting firm. With over 35,000 flight hours, Captain Angelo is recognized by many in his field as a SME and is on the list of universities and FAA organizations for his expertise. Captain Angelo is a writer of books as well as movie scripts, and he has several projects in development in the USA and Europe.

CPSIA information can be obtained
at www.ICGtesting.com
Printed in the USA
BVHW031259030621
608746BV00008B/27

9 781640 826458